Five

generations at work

Rebecca Robins
Patrick Dunne

Five
generations at work

How we win together, for good.

WILEY

This edition first published 2025

© 2025 Rebecca Robins and Patrick Dunne. All rights reserved.

Registered Office(s)
John Wiley & Sons, Inc., 111 River Street, Hoboken, NJ 07030, USA
John Wiley & Sons Ltd, The Atrium, Southern Gate, Chichester, West Sussex, PO19 8SQ, UK

Editorial Office
The Atrium, Southern Gate, Chichester, West Sussex, PO19 8SQ, UK

For details of our global editorial offices, customer services, and more information about Wiley products visit us at www.wiley.com.

Wiley also publishes its books in a variety of electronic formats and by print-on-demand. Some content that appears in standard print versions of this book may not be available in other formats. Designations used by companies to distinguish their products are often claimed as trademarks. All brand names and product names used in this book are trade names, service marks, trademarks or registered trademarks of their respective owners. The publisher is not associated with any product or vendor mentioned in this book.

Library of Congress Cataloging-in-Publication Data

Names: Robins, Rebecca (Writer of Five generations at work), author. |
 Dunne, Patrick (Writer of Five generations at work), author.
Title: Five generations at work : how we win together, for good / Rebecca
 Robins, Patrick Dunne.
Description: Hoboken, NJ, USA : Wiley, 2024. | Includes index.
Identifiers: LCCN 2024020963 (print) | LCCN 2024020964 (ebook) | ISBN
 9781394252206 (hardback) | ISBN 9781394252220 (adobe pdf) | ISBN
 9781394252213 (epub)
Subjects: Collaboration, innovation and productivity at work. Sustainable and systemic change.
Generational diversity
Classification: LCC HF5549.5.C75 R65 2024 (print) | LCC HF5549.5.C75
 (ebook) | DDC 658.30084/2—dc23/eng/20240603
LC record available at https://lccn.loc.gov/2024020963
LC ebook record available at https://lccn.loc.gov/2024020964

Cover Design by Jason Hyde
Author Photos: Courtesy of the Authors
Printed and bound by CPI Group (UK) Ltd, Croydon, CR0 4YY

C9781394252206_210824

Dedicated to my mother, Mary.

For your words and your wisdom – always.

With love, Rebecca

To my inspirational, resilient, incredibly
generous and joyful mum Margaret.

With love, Patrick

Contents

The rise of five generations in the workplace is colliding
with a world in flux – six decades of experience meet
a decade of force factors across climate, geopolitics,
technology and more. To solve for the realities and
unknowns of that flux, there is an urgent need to change
the prevailing discourse, from the default of divisive
generational silos and stereotypes to something much
more inspiring. Through evidence-based cases,
conversations and a call to action, we demonstrate how
to turn the dynamics and difference of generations into
more positively connected, collaborative and competitive
organisations.

Generations contribute unique perspectives, values, and
behaviours shaped by socio-economic, technological
and cultural factors. Connecting data across generations
and populations, we get behind the numbers of five
generations at work. Charting the big global data between
today and 2050, our intent is to widen and deepen our
perspective, showing the dramatic regional shifts that are
underway – and their implications for us all.

In conversation with:

Ahlström: *Collective impact*

Hoffmann-La Roche: *The 100-year view*

Mars: *The Power of Principles*

The Pentland Group: *The responsibility of ownership.*

6 Next Generation Boards

'Next generation boards' are emerging as a vital and valuable platform for progressing intergenerational dialogue within organisations. From a global body of research across corporates and non-profits, we demonstrate the business logic, and their potential for sustainable and systemic change.

Featuring insights from **Gucci**.

In conversation with:

The EY Foundation: *Head and Heart*

Mission 44: *Together, we're unstoppable.*

The FT: *Collaborate for success.*

Liberty Global: *Entrepreneurial energy*

7 Intergenerational Alliances

From public-private partnerships to collaborations across academia and industry, we examine the solutions-focused thinking and progressive work materialising through the different manifestations of intergenerational alliances.

Featuring insights from the **Samsung and UNDP partnership**, Generation17

In conversation with **Imaginable Futures:** *Invest for Success as Good Ancestors*

The St Gallen Symposium: *Lead with the next generation in mind.*

The EU Commission and Parliament: *Embracing the extremities*

Five Generations at Work is just the beginning of something much bigger – and it is not complete without a perspective on future generations. We unpack a world-first and some of the pioneering work that is actively encoding the lives of future generations, today.

Featuring insights from The **UN SDG Lab**

In conversation with **The Future Generations Act** (**Wales**): *Small and awesome*

Preface

We are at an unprecedented time in history, in the confluence of force factors of climate, geopolitics, technology and more. We are also witnessing firsts in both intergenerational and intragenerational shifts – the next decades will see the largest wealth transfer in history, and for the first time in history we have five generations at work.

And yet, narratives around generations have become warped and weaponised through bias and stereotypes. And this matters, as we are at an inflection point in the convergence of forces and flux that will challenge us, as businesses, as society – as humanity at large. We believe in, and evidence, a more productive and progressive approach – through turning labels into lenses, through seeing our human difference as a strength, and by the everyday actions that are making a difference and delivering sustainable change.

Written through the voices of five generations, which are celebrated and interwoven throughout, this book open-sources progressive and practical action, and what we can make happen through more inclusive ways of seeing, and more integrated ways of working.

You may be embarking on your first career. You may be a manager, or about to become one. You may be a founder, an owner, in a leadership role. You may have a plural or portfolio career. You may be first generation or taking on the work of other generations. The contexts are multiple, but they are united by the one dimension of diversity that we all share.

Rebecca Solnit, in addressing the crises and challenges of our times, said: *"Every crisis is in part a storytelling crisis. We are hemmed in by stories that prevent us from seeing, or believing in, or acting on the possibilities for change."*

The subtitle of *Five Generations at Work* is the pivot. It is about the possibilities for change.

Dear Reader

Here's to …

the connectors, the creators,
the first movers, the next movers,
the innovators, the integrators,
the interpreters and horizon scanners,
the generalists and the specialists,
the leaders, the managers and the owners.
Here's to us as individuals, as collectives, the world over.

This is dedicated to *you*. As one of the five generations at work, as someone who has a story, and a contribution. It is dedicated to every individual and collective behind the organisations featured in this book and so many more.

You may read this book word for word. You may read a few chapters. What matters is turning words into actions. We share work taking place across the world to inspire us to act on the **possibilities for change**. Because that is **how we begin to win together . . . for good.**

Thank you for your attention.
We would love to hear your story. Please get in touch . . .

"To stay human is to break a limitation."

Anne Carson

Anne Carson's writing defies easy definition. Her writing not only spans genres, but crosses genres. Her challenge around what it is to be human, and breaking the boundaries of genres, was one that we took on. We set out to break limitations in how we look at what defines us, and at what binds us across generations.

1

Introduction & Call to Action

The rise of five generations in the workplace is intersecting with the rise of exponential change. With the global advance of an ageing population, our workforces are operating across Silents, Boomers, Gen X, Millennials and Gen Z, with the advent of Gen Alpha on the horizon. What is striking is the simultaneous convergence and divergence – the convergence in the unprecedented moment of age diversity at work, and the divergence in the fractures and fragmentation exacerbated by the context of our times. In an age of flux, or as some have termed a 'polycrisis', the forces are being felt from the outfall of a pandemic to socio-political turbulence, from generative AI to the need to regenerate the planet. These multiple forces are rapidly changing the world of work, from the types of roles and shapes of our careers to the way in which we work together. Consequently, the knowledge, skills and behaviours needed to succeed are changing at a similar rate.

Yet the prevailing discourse on how different generations work together has defaulted into divisive generational silos and stereotypes. In the context of so much flux, and when it has never been more imperative to work together, we not only have a necessity to change this, but more importantly to transform it into a hopeful opportunity. For the first time in history companies have five generations in the workplace. And each generation has its own defining characteristics, values and attitudes shaped by the culture, technology and formative events of their time. In parallel, the pace of change in the workplace is accelerating, requiring adaptability from us all. As a consequence, the skills and behaviours necessary for how we win together are evolving. In valuing the human difference of each generation, we can rethink the dynamics of different generations as contributing to more connected, collaborative, and competitive organisations, drawing, rather than draining strength from multiple generations.

The indicators from leading global reports on the current and future state of generations, leadership and skills point consistently to the imperative of collaboration. Deloitte reports that only 6% of organizations believe their leaders understand how to effectively manage generational differences.[1] The value that effective multigenerational workforces can create across their talents, improving continuity and stability, assisting with the retention of critical skills and knowledge and a significant competitive advantage is further evidenced by The World Economic Forum (WEF) in *How a Multigenerational Workforce Is Key to Economic Growth*.[2] This also cites research on the age-inclusive workforce by the Organisation for Economic Co-operation and Development (OECD)[3]: *"Diversity of experience, generations and skills gives employers an important opportunity to harness the talent that different age groups bring to the workplace and improve productivity and profitability."*

Through a series of waves of research and our work over the past six years, we have amassed a global body of work and database on businesses, organisations and institutions who see generational diversity as a strength and are taking progressive action across generations. Underlying our research and this growing body of evidence is a consensus that we all, as individuals, collectives and organisations, have a greater capacity to thrive when we choose to turn generational labels into generational lenses, which are about learning from and with each other.

This is about breaking down silos and misperceptions on all aspects of generational equations. To do that, it will require unlearning of behaviours, it will need more empathy and understanding. The lazy discourse around generational differences has lost sight of the reality and recognition that there is value in the perspectives and experience of each generation, where no single generation has the prevailing monopoly.

With the fracturing of trust in institutions the world over, brands are stepping into the void, in some respects, in the mind of global consumers. There has never been a time for brands to establish more conscious and responsible roles, in business, and society and to demonstrate real progress from stated ambitions in diversity, ethics and sustainability, to systemic outcomes. Spanning intergenerational alliances, family businesses, next generation boards, intrapreneur platforms and deep commitments into future generations, this book demonstrates collaborative constructs that run counter to the divisive discourse that we seek to dismantle, exposing the counterpoint of generational tensions, with the urgency to regenerate – across business, society and the planet.

> **ΙΙWe live in an age of classification and I am not sure it's helping any of us.ΙΙ**
>
> Alex Mahon, Chief Executive of Channel 4

FROM LABELS TO LENSES

Ironically, in the context of so much tension-laden debate around generations, there is no standard determination of how we define a generation. *"As it stands, there is no official taxonomy or oversight committee who decide when a new generation starts or ends, or what to name it. Although these labels often evolve organically through popular media and public discourse, many originate from the Pew Research Center, a US Think Tank."*[4]

This naming and labelling is linked to our behavioural wiring to seek meaning in types and stereotypes. As Alex Mahon, Chief Executive of Channel 4 states in Channel 4's 2023 Beyond Z report: *"We live in an age of classification and I am not sure it's helping any of us."* A defining factor of our research and so many of the collectives that we talk with is the breaking of types, the challenging of so-called norms and an approach to measurement that is inherently more balanced and linked more to collective outcomes.

We set out the business logic for investing across the multigenerational workplace, as evidenced through our research across industries and global markets, with leading global brands, SMEs, founder and family businesses, institutions and non-profits. The structures on which many organisations have been established were forged in a different age, and not all are fit for purpose across the five generational workplace. Others have sprinted ahead and evolved more organically to embrace generational diversity and difference as both a more natural modus operandi and a distinct competitive advantage. In conversation across generations and across the world, we hear from five generations across students, first careers, mid careers, managers, leaders, owners, board members and wider partners.

MUTUAL LEARNING: BUILDING THE MINDSET AND MUSCLE OF LEADERSHIP

What we need are tomorrow's regenerative leaders – today. The stark reality is that we will miss the critical mass that we need unless we engage with this transitional era, in diversifying the pipeline of talent, and crucially, in building the mindset, skillset and toolkit. As The London Interdisciplinary School argues: *"The problems facing humanity are more complex, interconnected, and urgent than ever before. The modern workplace needs people who can tackle these kinds of issues and make a real impact on the world."*[5] The London Interdisciplinary School in the UK is amongst others across the world pioneering a new approach to higher education, where the curriculum is grounded not in subject matter verticals, but in the horizontal and zigzag connections of interdisciplinary thinking. As we shall go on to reinforce, the best working practice that we evidence is about shared value and outcomes – within and across generations. The skills required will converge around collaboration in new and deeper forms, around how to manage ambiguity and uncertainty, and, perhaps, one of the most important, yet underestimated skills – the ability to keep learning.

The shape and trajectory of careers are evolving and will change at an extraordinary pace, as are the skills needed to move with the pace of change, where singular disciplines of careers are becoming more multidisciplinary, where the linear verticals of career pathways are more fluid and cross-fertile. Putting a value on breadth and diversity of experience, and space for lateral exploration on our career paths, is the focus of David Epstein's prescient book: *Range: How Generalists Triumph in a Specialized World*. As the future of work is changing, and with it the shape of roles and the skills that we need, we must continue to adapt. The question is – are generations learning from each other, and are they working together effectively by putting their strengths to work? The cases that we share in the book are living examples of practical commitments to cultures of collaboration and lifelong learning.

One of the unintended consequences of change programmes or of ambitions to advance strategic agendas at work, has proven to be the tipping point of "project" or 'initiative' overload. Amongst that body of indicators, a survey by Gartner evidenced a steady decrease and drop in employee engagement with change initiatives in their organisations – from 74% in 2016 to 43% in 2022.[6]

This context is important for two reasons. First because the body of work that we share runs counter to this, defined by commitments that hardwire to business strategy, by doing fewer things well and through longer-term investment. In many cases this is about sustained and systemic change for how we look at rising leadership today for the leaders that we will need for the rising challenges in business and society. Second, because the overload effect of projects and initiatives – which are often disconnected and not sustained – is invariably a distraction from the real focus of building the muscle that is needed across all generations. The 'accidental manager' is a key case in point of this multigenerational muscle. The Chartered Management Institute (CMI) in the UK has been a longstanding voice on the consequences of accidental management, which speaks to the pervasive promotion into the title of manager without the important work on development and skills. The managerial role and responsibility that goes with it is of particular importance because it transcends generations.

Unpacking the benefits of intergenerational thinking and collaboration, we draw a future trajectory of the cumulative capability of how new generations of leadership demonstrate cultural and collaborative advantage, which, in turn, generates competitive advantage. Based on the common principles of collaborative, inclusive and respectful leadership, intergenerational thinking also establishes a mindset and skillset that offers an alternative to the 'heroic' narrative around leaders and leadership. This concept and context of superhero leadership is something that Margaret Heffernan, entrepreneur, author and professor of practice, addresses in calling out *"the enduring attraction of simplistic narratives."*[8] It brings to mind the words of Ken Frazier, former executive chairman and CEO of Merck, on how he shaped the culture at Merck: *"When a company is successful, the CEO gets a lot of credit for what I call the big moments, but leadership is in the many small, quiet moments with the team."* This is further supported by Rebecca Henderson in her book *Reimagining Capitalism in a World on Fire*: *"Real change happens in small rooms and in small actions that accumulate over time."*

> **"Intergenerational collaboration and leadership is a lifelong learning process to make transformation happen, everyone has a role to play and a wisdom to share from the experience of the age that we are at."**[7]
>
> Erioluwa Adeyinka
> Executive Director and Co-Founder, YouthxYouth, Nigeria

We explore living blueprints across cultures, disciplines, industries and generations that are *developing* both mindset and skillset, and empowering opportunities to exercise the muscle. Importantly, this is about no one 'ism' or defining solution. What we reflect is a lifecycle of intergenerational thinking – from platforms and programmes designed to represent and elevate the voices of next generations, to commitments designed to hardwire decision-making through the lenses of generations to come. This is also why we dedicate the culminating chapter to *future* generations. A powerful common pattern that emerges throughout is the **multiplier** effect through cohorts and generations. The work and ways of thinking that we are advocating today are the collective actions creating compound interest for tomorrow.

In the context of unprecedented forces across business and society, with far-reaching implications from one generation to the next, what emerges through intergenerational thinking is a deeper reflection on the age that we will have been a part of, and to which we will have contributed. One constant remains true – that humanity ever evolves through stages of its own progression and regression. We are part of generations past, with a responsibility for generations future, and it is easy for the generational discourse to forget the longer-term perspective of how we exist today has been informed and defined by the eras and movements before us – consider the references made today to a 'new Renaissance' that hark back to one of the most deeply formative times for humanity. In his book *Generations*,[9] Policy Expert at King's College London, Bobby Duffy brilliantly cites the Spanish philosopher José Ortega y Gasset, "*who believed that history was a series of epochs, where each new generation considered itself either heir to a valuable heritage or born to destroy it."* "*Ortega suggests that 'the concept of the generation is the most important one in the whole of history', precisely because it constitutes the mechanism by which 'history moves, changes, wheels and flows.'"*

Five Generations at Work is written through a series of multigenerational conversations and lenses for our multigenerational workplace. Importantly, we are not proposing another model or framework – each case study is a living blueprint from which we can all take insight and inspiration. Ultimately, this is a manifesto and movement for every generation, through the scale of change that generations can achieve *together*. We look through the lenses of five generations at work, from rising generations entering work for the first time, to generations in management and leadership positions, to generations at the edges of retirement. We hear from multiple generations within family businesses who are carrying forward the founding work of generations before them. We go inside the companies embedding generational thinking into their organisations. Some are establishing platforms for more productive dialogue across employees and leadership and enabling diverse pathways for more collaborative leadership. Others are mobilising ways to generate collaborative creativity and innovation across their organisation. We hear from those who are more proactively unlocking the accumulated experience of older generations and transferring that knowledge to rising generations. Through our focus on the 'five generations at work today', we identified a constant red thread throughout our research and conversations – on 'future generations'. We therefore dedicate our penultimate chapter to our longer-term legacy, as generations today, to the generations that have yet to be born, with a lens through the Seventh Generation principle.[10]

This book is about sharing the possibilities for us all, as individuals, as collectives, as organisations, when we engage with what we value in each other and why. As we hear in the chapter Intergenerational Alliances: "*The truth is that the greatest potential lies in combining the strengths of all age groups to create value that is greater than the sum of its parts.*"

What we go on to share, document and celebrate, is drawn from a diverse body of work, across family businesses, next generation boards, intrapreneurship, intergenerational alliances and investment in future generations.

2

Defining Our Generations

What do we mean by a generation, and what are the commonly used terms for different generations and why? As we have outlined, there is no definitive system for how generations come to be framed or named. There is something energising about this, suggesting an organic freedom where generational names are adopted, adapted and established through common use. It may also be the case that framing further evolves through how generations are seen as they age, and through their impact on the world.

Stereotypes, which tend to be oversimplified, biased and divisive, have become too pervasive. Indeed, one of the aims of this book is to challenge and break free from some of the stereotypes that have emerged around how different age groups might behave. Our perspective, and one shared and evidenced in our research and through this work, is that it is inherently more productive to think about generations in a series of ways, starting with, but by no means ending with age.

A definition that is often drawn on is from the seminal *Essays on the Sociology of Knowledge*: "*A generation can be defined as a group of individuals born within the same historical and socio-cultural context, who experience the same formative experiences and develop unifying commonalities as a result.*"[1]

In the West, the naming of generations tends to have been characterised by the conditions that a particular generation experienced and how they have responded to those conditions, as well as how they have behaved and influenced society, culture and subsequent generations. For example, the *"Lost"* generation in Europe, those who came of age during or just after World War I (1914–1918), were often viewed as cynical, disillusioned and without cultural or emotional stability. Hardly surprising given their horrific experiences and the social turmoil that they lived through as a result of a war which killed over 20 million, left another 20 million physically injured, with countless others suffering mental health injuries. There may be other manifestations of this in those currently suffering the consequences of wars. There are echoes of it in what we are seeing in the impact of a pandemic.

In Asia and in Africa the situation is a lot more complex due to the very different histories of the countries within those regions. In some Asian nations, including China, Vietnam and Korea, generational names can be more literal with a common character, often the first or second, embedded in a person's given name to identify which generation they are from, with siblings and cousins sharing that character. For example, in Chinese the symbol 庆 meaning Qing links Wang Qingzhao with Wang Qingxi.

The first of South Africa's *"Born Free"* generation, those born after the end of the apartheid era in 1994, may have felt, but not understood, the vibrancy of the early years of Mandela's rainbow nation as small children. As teenagers and young adults, they will have felt the consequences of the challenging time which has followed under subsequent presidents and its impact upon the economy, and on the opportunities and the quality of life in their country. As a South African friend of ours put it many of the *"Born Frees"* have sadly and ironically become trapped and are now better described as the *'Frustration Generation'*.

In China, the government's 1979 to 2015 One-Child policy has also influenced the behaviour of around 180 million Millennials who also coincided with the economic re-awakening of the country. This is sometimes described as the 4-2-1 generation – four grandparents, two parents and one child, to whom all the attention and money flows, combined with no need to share, which has had an impact. It will also have a future impact as it reverses to a 1-2-4 with one Millennial having to support older family members.

In Vietnam the 9X generation, those born in the 1990s, followed the post-war generation of people born in the aftermath of the war ending in 1975. They overlapped, and have much in common, with older Millennials elsewhere in the world. Yet, the biggest influence on them was likely to be the opening up of Vietnam to the rest of the world, especially through the internet and the profound and rapid development of its economy.

The concept of identifying and labelling distinct groups of people based on shared experiences and cultural influences emerged as societies underwent significant transformations. As the attributes for various generations will differ, and different societies may approach generational distinctions in various ways, **we can distil four force factors shaping generational mindset and behaviour: Economic; Social and cultural; Technological and Conflict.** It is also likely that these generational mindsets and behaviours will adapt and develop as these force factors influence them through their key stages of life.

The classic names of generations in the West in the last century or so have been the *"Lost", "Greatest", "Silent",*

"Baby Boomers", *"Gen X"*, *"Gen Y"* more commonly known as *"Millennials"*, *"Gen Z"* and the latest *"Gen Alpha"*. Variations on some of the generational names emerged in the context of more recent generations. This even gave rise to hybrid naming such as Xennials, speaking to a cross-over of a 'micro-generation' at the confluence of Gen X and Millennials.

Generation	Born Between	% Global Population	Why so Called?
Boomers	1946–1964	13%	Born from the boom in birth rates amongst relevant countries at the end of World War II and the resultant economic boom.
Gen X	1965–1980	18%	Popularised by Canadian author Douglas Coupland in his novel "Generation X: Tales for an Accelerated Culture." As the undefined letter, X was embraced by a generation who did not want to be defined as previous generations had been.
Millennials	1981–1996	23%	Originally named Gen Y to follow Gen X, Millennials became the more popular descriptor as the older members of this generation were reaching adulthood at the turn of the century.

Generation	Born Between	% Global Population	Why so Called?
Gen Z	1997– 2012	25%	This is the first generation of digital natives. In China they are also thought of as the generation who grew up in the midst of the nation's economic re-awakening, whereas in Japan they are defined as much by difficult economic conditions as they are by age.
Gen Alpha	2013 and still being born	18%	A naming convention has taken effect in the circularity of the alphabet. Whether that evolves remains to be seen, as this generation rises with the rise of generative AI.

We have intentionally used a consensus of sources in framing the age of generations, in the spirit of reflecting the degree of fluidity. And with Silents still present in the workforce, the Gen Alpha to Boomer range also correlates with the core of the five generations that will be at work, as we go on to map the shape shifts in population data. Those shifts will be important to keep in mind as we look ahead to our collective responsibility today in our culminating chapter on *Generations Future*.

Our stated focus is on how different generations are interacting at work, and how we can move away from the current divisive, stereotype-fuelled discourse to something which positively harnesses the power of both their differences and diversity. In essence a move from an *"Other"* mindset to a *"Together"* mindset. It is a mindset that we believe is fundamental to overcome the major challenges that we face in business, society, climate and geopolitics, and is integral to a more collaborative and inclusive leadership skillset.

> *"In essence a move from an "Other" mindset to a "Together" mindset."*

Boomers

Boomers are now in their sixties and seventies, and, in many respects, their *direct* influence in the workplace is declining. Their *indirect* influence however remains strong in a number of ways – with many acting as advisors, investors or board members. The natural decline in the numbers of Boomers, as they were retiring from the workplace, was also given further impetus by the pandemic – from those who sadly lost their lives to many who left the workforce for good, and others returning to it in part-time rather than full-time roles. In late 2021, for example, an over 3 million additional retirees in the US was reported over what might have been expected.[2]

Gen X

Gen X may not yet have drawn the same attention as Boomers and Millennials but this may change. Gen Xers have a lot of executive power and have taken over from Boomers in key leadership roles and holding responsibility across all generations in the workplace. The majority of Fortune 500 CEOs were 43–58 years old at the time of writing.[3]

The financial pressures on this generation are also set in another context. According to the National Institute on Retirement Security in the US: *"Most Gen Xers, regardless of race, gender, marital status or income, are failing to meet retirement savings targets."* The implications of this pressure means that any current squeeze that many Gen Xers feel is likely to become even more pronounced affecting confidence and preparedness to take risk. This is even without the risk of Artificial Intelligence (AI) replacing many traditional jobs in a wide range of professions. It is already materialising that some Gen Xers have either anticipated this or have seized the opportunity to go plural and fractional early.

Millennials

The most talked about generation are now no longer the largest generation in population terms, with those now in their late twenties to early forties, representing 23% of the world's population and Gen Z's 25%. However, Millennials are likely to be the largest generation in the workforce. According to the World Economic Forum (WEF) report in 2021, noted above, *"Of all generations Millennials are the most educated."* At the same time, as the FT's John Burn-Murdoch noted *". . . this hasn't translated into economic success in the way that it has for past generations."*[4] Another striking statistic in the WEF report is that: *"Asia is home to a quarter of the global Millennial population and Millennials hold two thirds of passports in China."* The WEF report also noted that *"Millennials control 65% of Africa's purchasing power through household purchases, valued at $845 billion."*

As with every generation, it has its own challenges. Deloitte's 2023 Gen Z and Millennial Survey[5], which connected with 14,483 Gen Zs and 8383 Millennials across 44 countries, provides an excellent summary of these challenges. Only 62% of Millennials say that work is central to their identity which is already 26% higher than Gen Zs. Only one-third of Millennials are very satisfied with their work/life balance. And three-quarters of Millennial respondents would consider looking for a new job if their employer asked them to go on site full time. The indication, for many, is that expectations and aspirations, whether Gen Z or Millennial, are not being met.

Gen Z

Spanning adolescence to mid-twenties, Gen Zs are already in work or on the cusp of their first experiences in the workplace. The Deloitte 2023 Gen Z and Millennial Survey provides some helpful context. First that *"46% of Gen Zs in the survey have taken on either part or full time paying jobs in addition to their primary role"* and this is a growing trend. The most popular side hustles and additional jobs are cited as: *"Selling products or service online (21%), engaging in gig work (20%), pursuing artistic ambitions (18%) and social media influencing (16%)."* When you look at the motivations apart from money for doing this, the second highest for Gen Zs is that it is driven by passion and purpose.

Gen Alpha

Gen Alphas will be entering an employment market and a world shaped by the ramifications of the significant flux that we are living through today. Apart from the major geopolitical upheavals and technological shifts, especially with AI, many will have already experienced a major disruption to their education and social development through the pandemic. Will some of these forces result in them emerging as the most adaptive generation yet?

Generations in the Workforce

Putting the multigenerational workforce into context was integral to our work, and to the work that we will be unpacking and sharing. Seeking to understand how the demographics might shift and influence the dynamics in the world of work, we studied the big data around generations in the workforce, with the tremendous support of our good friends Jeff Jordan and Toshiko Kaneda at the Population Reference Bureau in Washington, DC.

Definitions of working age tend to be based on the laws pertaining to each country and vary around the world. In most countries there is no norm in age at which it is mandated to stop working, although there may be ages at which it is a requirement in certain professions. Where relevant, it tends to be driven by the age at which the state pension can start to be accessed. The Organisation for Economic Co-operation and Development (OECD) uses 15–64 years old as its working-age definition. As an aside, we think this age range needs updating to reflect the reality in many countries where people are now working productively well into their seventies because they can, need to, or want to.

The type and volume of work is another question entirely. For many it will be influenced and impacted by the rise of generative AI, whether in its potential to displace hundreds of millions of jobs in the near future, or to create large numbers of higher paid, better quality jobs. While these numbers have yet to play out, let us take a look at the big data that we do have better purchase on, adding important context to understanding how the generational shape of populations is evolving.

Looking at our global population today of just over 8 billion people, the Population Pyramids below show the split by generation and gender. We will go on to chart the same for Africa, Asia, Europe and the Americas to show the projected shift in proportion of that population between 2023 and 2050 by age, generation and gender. This is to help us to understand that change and, importantly, to inspire us to think about the implications of these shifts, both at a global and regional level.

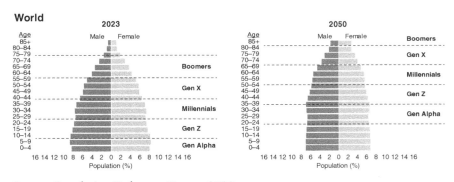

Source: Population Reference Bureau 2023

As the world population charts evidence, in 2023 our 8 billion global population looks reasonably evenly distributed by age until people reach their mid-fifties. The UN projects the global population to rise by over 20% to reach 9.7 billion by 2050 and to continue to rise, albeit more slowly, reaching 10.4 billion in 2100. The UN also projects average longevity will be up 6% from 2019 to 77.2 years old in 2050.[6] Note that the data is for those people living in the region, that the gender data available is categorised as male or female, and that use of the male/female descriptors is contingent on the data that is available. Different government statistical offices categorise gender differently and are continuing to evolve their approaches.

The topic of most interest to us in the trend data is what is happening to the mix of generations in the workplace over the next decades and the rise of new generations. The chart below gives us a good indication. By 2050 the youngest Boomers, Gen Xers, Millennials, Gen Zs and Gen Alphas will be 86, 70, 54, 38 and 25, respectively. Globally, the five generations will look reasonably balanced for the rest of this decade, with the proportion of Gen Xers forecast to fall significantly from there. As ever with aggregate or average statistics, this masks very different dynamics by region as we shall go on to unpack.

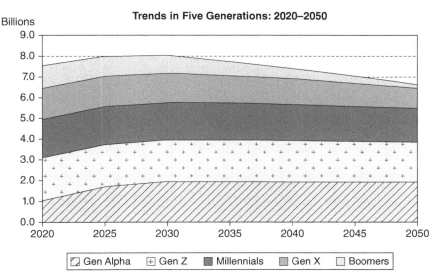

Source: Population Reference Bureau 2023

REGIONAL PERSPECTIVES AND IMPLICATIONS

Africa, Asia, Europe and the Americas, according to the Population Reference Bureau (PRB), account for over 99% of the global population today and, according to the World Bank, produce over 90% of the world's $100 trillion Gross Domestic Product.[7] As the Pyramids demonstrate, the distribution and age of populations within some regions is expected to shift significantly and in very different ways.

The picture of what is happening in different regions and the projected data is valuable context-setting for how we better understand the shape and shifts of generations – the differences are striking and have significant implications for the balance and dynamics of generations at work.

Africa

The picture for Africa is the most striking of all regions. Set in context with the shapes of the other regions, which have experienced, or are in the process of, significant ageing, Africa's population is the youngest. Africa is also set to shape shift significantly by 2050. With the African population growing by over 1 billion by 2050 and ageing in many major populations elsewhere by 2050, 25% of the world's population will be African compared with 18% today. In West Africa, Nigeria's population alone is forecast to increase by 69% by 2050, to reach 378 million. Nigeria's story is significant, as one of the five countries in Sub-Saharan Africa projected to contribute 50% of the growth in the world's working age population (ages 15–64) starting in the early 2040s.

At this stage, it is hard to predict whether growth in jobs will keep pace with this due to a number of factors, not

Africa

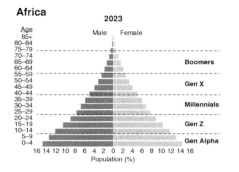

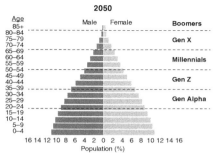

The Americas

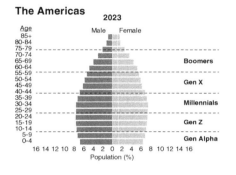

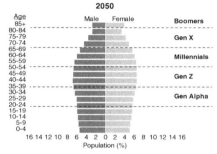

Asia

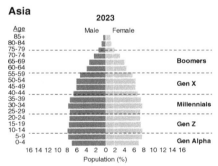

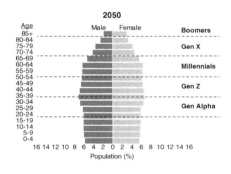

Europe

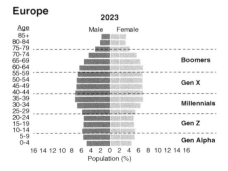

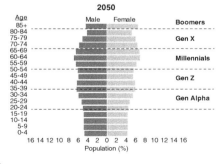

Source: Population Reference Bureau 2023

Defining Our Generations

least in education. Work done by Education Sub-Saharan Africa (ESSA) has shown that the tertiary sector (Universities and Colleges) is significantly under-resourced even for today's population. Urgent policy changes will be required to meet capacity and capability demands for the surge in population already underway. As the tertiary sector trains teachers, midwives, and many skills needed for work and to support successful economies and societies, tertiary education investment should be at the forefront of change in both working practices and maximising the value of multigenerational workforces.[8]

The Americas

The demographic dynamic in the Americas contrasts sharply with that in Africa. The population, which is already considerably older than in Africa and Asia, is forecast to be driven by the ageing of the three biggest generations, the Boomers, Gen Xers and Millennials. Projections chart the continued growth of older workers (65+) over the next decade, with older adults accounting for 57% of overall growth of the workforce (those working and looking for work).[9]

This shift is significant, as we go on to unpack, with organisations thinking differently about the value of older adults in the workforces, and importantly, connecting it into transferable experience and knowledge across generations.

Asia

Accounting for 59% of the World's population in 2023, the trajectory of Asia's population influences the global balance. China and India, with populations of 1.4 and

1.3 billion, respectively, are the dominant countries accounting for 59% of the Asian population (in a curious symmetry with the world percentage). China's population is currently predicted to fall by 7% by 2050, and India will move from decades of high growth to peaking in the 2050s and falling from there. South Korea, officially the Republic of Korea, a much smaller country with a population of 52 million, recently announced the lowest birth rate in the world.[10] All of this has major implications for the economies, political environment and balance of generations in the workforce in these countries. Yet the populations of other nations within the region, for example Indonesia and Vietnam, are still projected to grow significantly by 2050 (14% and 9% respectively) and will have a very different dynamic and generation balance in their workforces. Indeed, Indonesia is set to become the world's sixth-largest economy by 2027.[11]

Europe

Europe's generational balance in 2023 looks very different to that in Africa, Asia or the US with a proportionately older population, as the flattened levels of the pyramid show. The shift to 2050 is projected to be dramatic for Europe in a different way to that in Africa. Europe is ageing fast, and its population is projected to fall by 2050, with the working-age population projected to decline by 7 million from its level in 2022 to 258 million by 2030.[12] The projected shape of the demographic in 2050 is striking with the younger age bands shrinking. To put it into real terms, the proportion of the European population under age 10 is projected to be only around a third of that in Africa.

"That there will be generational flux for some time to come is evident. Importantly, we need to find ways to acknowledge that flux positively, make the most of the talents and experiences of our different generations and to be supportive across generations."

Summary

So, what can we draw from these numbers, and what does this mean for today's generations in the workforce? The projection for Asia, the Americas and Europe is that they will evolve into more evenly distributed mixes of generations at work, with the exception of the youngest generations which the charts suggest are shrinking – Korea and Japan are two clear examples of this. By 2050, the impact of technology may well be a significant factor in reducing the number of people needed to be in work, but in the near-term older generations in these regions may need to stay in work longer. In Africa the challenge is more about job creation as its working-age population is projected to increase significantly in the coming decades.

That there will be generational flux for some time to come is evident. Importantly, we need to find ways to acknowledge that flux positively, make the most of the talents and experiences of our different generations and to be supportive across generations. Not to do so misses a tremendous opportunity for us all economically, socially and for our planet.

We have looked at what we mean by a generation as well as how the definitions of generations form and norm over time. Unpacking the big numbers on generations in the world at large and in the workforce opened up a wider perspective on how we think about our roles, our careers and our identities, in the context of regional lenses that have very different stories to tell.

The core of *Five Generations at Work* hardwires on its very call to action - *How we win together, for good* - focusing on case studies and conversations across industries, organisations and cultures that demonstrate the practicalities, potential and multiple advantages of inclusive and progressive work across generations. But first, we need to engage with the realities of the divisive discourse that has emerged, and its implications and challenges in the five generational workplace. To channel the words of Anne Carson, we need to break the limitations.

*"There is a crack, a crack in everything.
That's how the light gets in."*

Leonard Cohen

This timeless lyric is from Cohen's album *The Future* and the song *Anthem*. We celebrate the difference in every one of us that makes us 'us', and the magic of what happens **when we let the light in.**

3

Intergenerational Working

As we were undertaking our research and looking to further explore and understand the challenges of inter-generational working, we took a diversity of approaches. In practice, this meant:

> *Conducting a global body of research with a wide range of organisations facing different challenges and exploring their approaches to managing multigenerational work-places.*
>
> *Taking pulses into the generational discourse through non-generative AI-based research and super-analytics.*
>
> *Paralleling these two paths with a series of conversations around the world, and deep reflection upon our own experiences and work across a diverse range of international organisations and roles.*

As we travelled, we built a live database of evidence of our ongoing research and reflections across global markets looking for patterns and, most importantly, at how people were pioneering new ways of working together across generations. One of those new ways of working relates to the use of AI and our own use of it in the research for this book. With our partners Quilt.AI and Anurag Banerjee's talented team, we took a multigenerational and multicultural approach to the design and implementation of the study, working with a diverse team of Gen Zs, Millennials, Gen Xers and Boomers from five countries.

Our approach was to deploy deep anthropological AI expertise combined with significant experience of leading and working with multigenerational organisations of different sizes and scales, and what we were learning from our interviews and case studies. Combining this with our ongoing research enabled us to tap into insights and experiences across generations, and discussion of practical solutions and approaches to the many common challenges that are widely faced in working together intergenerationally. A selection of these solutions and approaches is profiled in depth in our conversations and case studies, and we have drawn from a few of them here to show examples of the shift from challenges to change.

The Challenges

So, what are these challenges, and what is it that so many of us are trying to solve for?

Three fundamental challenges emerge for organisations and individuals around the world when working intergenerationally. There may be a multitude of ways in which they might be expressed, but as we continued to stress-test them, it kept coming back to these three fundamentals:

1. Understanding each other
2. Communicating with each other and
3. Maximising our collective potential through our individual difference

They go hand in hand with a fourth challenge, which was a major motivator for us to write this book: escaping the divisive discourse around generations. A discourse which constrains thinking and possibilities, positivity and collaboration.

The memes that have evolved characterising different generations are all too often projected onto a whole generation, fail to recognise the diversity within generations and often ignore the facts. Other common negative elements of the current discourse are that younger generations are work-shy, have unrealistic expectations and a greater sense of entitlement than previous generations, whereas the Boomers have stolen the economic futures of younger generations and have also destroyed the planet. Bobby Duffy's book *Generations* unpicks many of these claims and sums the situation up well by remarking that *"Phoney generational stereotypes are feeding a phoney generational war"* and that *"inequality is an increasingly intergenerational issue"* that is not confined to any single generation.[1] Indeed a 2023 study from the Institute of Fiscal Studies stated that *"In the UK 48% of the roughly 812,500 50–70 year olds who retired in 2020–21 are living in poverty."*[2]

Our title, *Five Generations at Work,* was a collaborative and purposeful call to action driven by how urgently we need to press the reset button on this discourse to enable us to refresh our thinking about other generations and how we work together. To achieve this, we need to understand the challenges better, see the opportunities more clearly and find the motivation to lead and work together in more collaborative ways.

Understanding each other

Misunderstanding is a common cause of conflict and is an underlying feature of much of the media coverage on intergenerational frustrations. Not understanding why someone has said something or behaved in a certain way can easily undermine confidence and trust on both sides of the conversation. Common causes of misunderstanding between generations are often multidimensional, related to insufficient knowledge, a lack of shared experiences, differing values, expectations, motivations, working styles and the way we communicate as well as natural gravitation towards our own generation. All of these have the potential to inhibit or negatively charge conversations, compounding the problem.

How many leadership teams know what the demographics of their organisations are, measure churn by age group and understand both their specific intergenerational challenges and opportunities? Having more tangible purchase on this context, as illustrated through our conversations with the EU Commission & Parliament, can inform thinking, catalyse action and provide the basis for measuring the impact of different strategies and tactics. The power balance between employers and employees can also affect attitudes. The balance of supply and demand overall, as well as for specific skills and experiences, is another factor. Sectoral and regional shifts in employment also have a part to play. Whether you come from regions abundant or scarce in relevant employment opportunities makes a difference to how you perceive the labour market and vice versa for employers.

Another important aspect of context relates to the nature of the organisations that we are working in. This is why we segmented our research to ensure that we covered different organisational contexts in terms of sector, place, scale and form of ownership. We were also interested in differences between and within the commercial and social sectors as well as governments. Family businesses, naturally, also have a special place when considering multigenerational workforces, as we go on to unpack in deeper conversations with family members across four very different businesses.

Communication

Thinking about the dimensions of difference, in how we communicate, make decisions, give and receive feedback, persuade, trust and so on is helpful. The same approach can be taken when considering generational differences. Erin Meyer's insightful book *The Culture Map* provides a framework for understanding, and approaches to managing, cultural differences in the workplace. She debunks the unhelpful nature of stereotypes in favour of cultural norms, which help us understand better why people may feel and behave differently through the lens of culture. There is relevance and resonance here in how we think about intergenerational differences.

Communication tools and channels can be a specific source of tension, bridging or exacerbating the gap in how employees experience their understanding of, and engagement with, the organisation. It is becoming ever more challenging to find communication and social platforms of universal appeal that meet the many requirements of organisations and individuals for the wide range of purposes required. Especially with regard to confidentiality and privacy. As a result, many organisations are using numerous platforms and channels of communications and relying on customers, employees and other stakeholders to simply use their channel of choice. Increased levels of virtual working accelerated by the pandemic are also likely to have increased the challenge in decreasing the potential for osmotic learning, often so critical in better understanding of our colleagues, and in gaining and giving feedback.

Understanding difference may be a pre-requisite for working more effectively together, but it is not sufficient. We also need to be positively motivated to want to manage whatever that difference is, and we need to have the communication and broader skills to help us achieve it in practice.

The FT's John Burn-Murdoch casts a spotlight on something that is happening at an *intra*generational level. Examining generational world views, he charts the rise of gender divisions within Gen Z. *"One of the most well-established patterns in measuring public opinion is that every generation tends to move as one in terms of its politics and general ideology. Its members share the same formative experiences, reach life's big milestones at the same time and intermingle in the same spaces. So how should we make sense of reports that Gen Z is hyper-progressive on certain issues, but surprisingly conservative on others? The answer, in the words of Alice Evans, a visiting fellow at Stanford University and one of the leading researchers on the topic, is that today's under-thirties are undergoing a great gender divergence, with young women in the former camp and young men the latter. Gen Z is two generations, not one."*[3]

John Burn-Murdoch cites a wave of examples showing the expanding gender gap across liberal and conservative world views in Europe. In South Korea that gap has already grown to a chasm. He continues: *"In the country's*

2022 presidential election, while older men and women voted in lockstep, young men swung heavily behind the right-wing People Power party, and young women backed the liberal Democratic party in almost equal and opposite numbers. Korea's is an extreme situation, but it serves as a warning to other countries of what can happen when young men and women part ways. Its society is riven in two. Its marriage rate has plummeted, and birth rate has fallen precipitously, dropping to 0.78 births per woman in 2022, the lowest of any country in the world." What we are witnessing is not only divides between generations, but within a generation.

Our three ways of exploring the practical solutions that organisations were adopting in the context of wider ideological shifts, led to a major conclusion. In trying to solve a problem we discovered a bigger opportunity. Reducing friction was part of the generational dynamics, and the bigger opportunity had become to demonstrate how we can maximise individual and collective potential and look for ways to enhance motivation, capabilities and performance. Through our research, and in conducting the interviews and case studies, we had many inspiring moments and could clearly see the difference in companies who were engaging directly with generational dynamics in different ways. Denoising the divisive discourse and focussing on positive, pragmatic and progressive work might provide something more motivating and meaningful for everyone – whether a student making their first career move, to managers, to leadership teams, with relevance for companies and organisations across cultures and industries.

Motivation has been at the centre of much of the commentary on intergenerational difference, one that has manifested too often in a reductive and divisive way. We believe it would be far more productive to think about how we maximise the potential of our organisations through making the most of the diversity of different generations through positive motivation. Throughout our lives one of the common experiences that we both share is how much we thrive on interacting with different generations – learning from them, enjoying their company and gaining inspiration from all ages. We met through the EY Foundation, which, as can be seen from the case study in Next Generation Boards, is a strong example of the power of intergenerational collaboration amongst five generations.

Motivational experts often categorise motivation into intrinsic or extrinsic. Intrinsic is where we do something because we enjoy it, extrinsic is where we are motivated by the promise of some form of reward. Our motivation has been both intrinsic and extrinsic – we get a lot of joy from working with those from different generations and cultures as well as knowing that it enriches our capabilities, knowledge and ability to lead. In summary, working effectively with those from different generations will bring its own rewards as well as increase our individual and collective performance and potential.

For some, it may start as extrinsic motivation. We do it because we know it will lead to rewards, and the intrinsic motivation may need to be developed. It can then develop into intrinsic because the knowledge, skills, behaviours and confidence we gain, usually through a mix of experience, through formal leadership development and the role modelling of others makes it enjoyable. At a family level the classic example of a grandparent conveying a piece of wisdom to a grandchild and the child achieving something because of the wisdom of an elder is uplifting. As is the expression of a grandparent who gains a fresh new insight from a grandchild. The workplace equivalents of these moments of learning from each other, getting through tricky situations, mastering new skills and thriving from each other's company, can be hugely motivational as well as improve the performance of the organisation.

"The context makes it imperative that we draw upon the collective power of our generations."

Maximising our collective potential through our individual differences

There is an enduring attraction and human interest in conflict and division between generations. It has long been part of the popular media and literature diet in all its forms, from light comedy to film noir, and we can trace its imprint back through ancient history. The advent and growth of social media have brought many advantages in connecting people from different generations and providing access to a wider range of views than traditional media channels may have provided. Yet, it also makes it easier, cheaper and faster to polarise views on important issues and to promote unsubstantiated views as fact.

We can choose to accept these narratives and let them continue to spiral, or we can do something to positively influence a more constructive narrative and course of individual and collective action. The fundamental mission is to find ways to reduce the frictions and maximise the value of the differences. The first step is to acknowledge the friction and difference – inertia only risks exacerbating the challenges. The ultimate job of a leader is to achieve the organisation's vision. Simply reducing tensions at work alone is unlikely to enable them to achieve that vision. It is also profoundly unambitious and misses a big opportunity. To harness the creativity that comes from the diversity of perspectives from different generations, to better understand our markets, to adopt and successfully deploy innovative ideas, to increase our resilience and sustainability, while having more fun doing so is more practical and productive. To navigate and succeed will require creativity, ingenuity, wisdom and bravery. The context of our times makes it imperative that we draw upon the collective power of our generations.

> **"Collaboration that is essential to drive the SDGs needs to be much deeper, wider, and stronger."**
>
> Dr. Ed Brooks, The Oxford Character Project

The quest for innovation as well as the necessity of having to respond to disruption and volatility appear to have been key stimulants of cross-generational initiatives for many organisations. Unsurprisingly, this has meant that organisations have been more curious, open to learning and continuously adapting their approaches. A good example of this is LVMH DARE!, as we detail in our chapter *The Intrapreneurial Mindset*. The spark for the creation of what has become an intrapreneurial movement within luxury goods giant LVMH (owner of brands such as Louis Vuitton, Dior and Tiffany), was the ambition of Laetitia Roche-Grenet and a conversation with Pascal Jouvin. Pascal, who leads LVMH House and programmes for high potential and top management, had an interest in maximising Laetitia's potential and had listened to the motivations around her next move within the company. What resulted was Laetitia's realisation of the platform DARE – Disrupt, Act, Risk to be an Entrepreneur! As you will see, it has been an extraordinary success.

Turning a greater ambition into a practical reality

As with many realities of leadership, and with organisational change more generally, the most substantial challenge is often not in understanding why change might be good for the organisation, but rather *how* to gain the alignment, resources and commitment necessary from others to turn our ideas and good intentions into successful realities. So, if we want to maximise the individual and collective potential of multiple generations in the workplace, how can we make it happen?

There are fundamentals needed for any organisation to take a big step forward in maximising the potential of multiple generations in the workplace. Reflecting on our experiences, the body of work from across the world, our interviews, case studies and the AI research led us to some clear conclusions about those fundamentals:

- An ambitious vision, strategy and plan which is integral to that of the organisation overall and its operating model.
- A collaborative style of leadership with a genuine commitment from the board and leadership team to maximise potential and invest in employee growth across all generations.

- An enabling and reinforcing culture which is strong on Collaboration, Respect, Inclusivity, Leadership and Innovation.
- The resources, processes and governance to match all of the above.

The driving purpose of any multigenerational workforce strategy and the actions that go with it should be hardwired to the organisation's overarching vision, strategy, culture and performance objectives and ideally additive to its operating model.

Analysing the demographics, motivations, attitudes and engagement of the existing workforce amongst different generations and looking at what other organisations are doing will inform the approach. It may also help to raise ambitions, as well as identify specific opportunities. Moreover, doing this provides both a baseline and the mechanisms to chart progress and impact, and to feed continuous learning and improvement.

Ambition matters. The success of LVMH's DARE – Disrupt, Act, Risk to be an Entrepreneur! – engaging thousands of staff across generations is a good example of greater ambition paying off. DARE has enabled a very large business to ensure that as it scales further its entrepreneurial gene not only survives but thrives and drives performance.

> **"Our culture of curiosity is an important binding element for us."**
>
> Chiara Tamburini, The EU Parliament

The EY Foundation's vision to have young people *"At the head and heart"* of the organisation in order to achieve its overall vision is another good example. Embedding that in its vision and governance through its Youth Advisory Board and having young people on the main board, as described in Next Generation Boards, has deeply embedded this principle and driven significant social impact.

Collaborative leadership

Importantly, the motivations for the commitments of both the EY Foundation and LVMH were about more than reducing friction. They were also driven by the desire to achieve the overarching vision of the respective organisations, and they have both been fuelled by diversity of thought and creative tension. Each required investment and a pioneering risk-taking spirit involving challenges along the way, and, with shared ambition and a collaborative spirit, both are achieving their goals.

They also required a collaborative style of leadership and a genuine commitment from the Board and leadership team to both maximise potential and minimise the friction. There are a variety of descriptions of collaborative leadership. The description provided by The King's Fund, a Healthcare Foundation which works collaboratively with health system organisations, is powerful for its clarity and practicality: *"Collaborative leadership is grounded in the belief that a shared model of leadership is more creative and effective than a leader or group of staff working alone. Sometimes leaders will adopt a collaborative leadership approach when working with their peers; in other instances, a leader focuses on creating the conditions that mean others can collaborate well."* The last sentence is particularly relevant and links to the importance of culture.

According to the Oxford Character Project's survey of business values, covering 221 leading organisations in the UK, collaboration is the most frequently stated value (Oxford Character Project, 2022). Led by Dr. Ed Brooks at the University of Oxford, The Oxford Character Project has been exploring the relationship between character, culture and leadership in business since 2020. Within an illuminating body of evidence, their research and analysis has pointed to the connection of collaboration with: diversity and inclusion, partnership, belonging, supportiveness, respect, openness and trust.

As Dr. Ed Brooks explains what emerged through the study, "*Companies recognise the value of fostering team cultures that exhibit high levels of psychological safety, enabling people to contribute candidly and creatively. They also seek to build strong external partnerships in order to exchange expertise and address shared challenges. However, while many companies link collaboration to business performance, only a small number explicitly connect collaboration and social purpose. Companies do show such collaboration at times of crises—the cooperation of rival firms in the Ventilator Challenge during the COVID pandemic is a great example—but mindsets need to reach beyond profit to purpose to make such collaboration more common. This is where responsible leadership and virtues, such as justice, courage, purpose, and hope, can be combined to create high-impact collaboration.*

"Character is central to the development of responsible management and leadership in business, which is an important pillar of the work of the United Nations to achieve the

Sustainable Development Goals (UN PRME, Principles of Responsible Management Education 2023). It is relatively easy to collaborate between people on the same team, especially when there is a short-term return. Collaboration that is essential to drive the SDGs needs to be much deeper, wider, and stronger. Its success depends on leaders with the moral muscles of intentionally cultivated virtues who can bring diverse communities together to achieve the most important goals."

The basic need to collaborate was powerfully put by Imaginable Futures, the social impact investor focused on education in Brazil, Sub-Saharan Africa and the US which is profiled in our chapter Intergenerational Alliances. *"We have a history at odds with our future and therefore we need to collaborate if we are to shift injustices and dismantle barriers so that all learners can thrive."* The importance of creating the conditions that mean others can collaborate well with all generations was illustrated in a highly pragmatic way by Chiara Tamburini from the European Parliament: *"It's important that everyone in a management role is able to relate, to inspire, motivate and manage people no matter what generation they are from, just as with any other form of diversity."*

There was another interesting aspect of the culture of the two connected large multigenerational and multicultural organisations that make up the EU Parliament and EU Commission that we learned more about, in the emphasis on their *"Culture of curiosity"* and how this enables more organic collaboration between all its staff. *"Our culture of curiosity, which we share with the*

Commission, is an important binding element for us. We are, and have been, since our formation, a highly multicultural workforce, where people are inherently curious and interested in our different cultures, languages and perspectives. It's very organic." Intended to bond and bind the organisations across different nations, its unifying characteristics have also proven effective across different generations.

The extraordinary St Gallen Symposium is a leading embodiment of cross-generational collaboration and was born out of the conflict and years of generational tension arising in street protests in Europe in the 1960s. The greater empathy and understanding that they have fostered have also sparked collaboration and innovation, such as the New Generational Contract described in the chapter Intergenerational Alliances.

At a more fundamental level, training and development, team-building events, performance and feedback processes and mutual mentoring programmes delivered through a multigenerational lens are important contributors. Mutual mentorship has a helpful role to play in building empathy and understanding, and showed up consistently in positive terms in the AI research and in our interviews and case studies. The tag *"Mutual mentoring"* recognises an evolution not only from the classic mentoring of a junior or younger person by someone more experienced, but also from the *reverse mentoring* which has become more prevalent. *Mutual mentoring* takes the exchange into a space where it is acknowledged that both learn from each other. Online commentary from all generations places emphasis on the importance of the quality of execution of these programmes, including demand for more training on how to be an effective mentor.

These commitments are an important element in the mix and, used smartly, can foster collaboration and continuous learning across all generations. Mission 44, the charitable foundation set up by Formula One champion Sir Lewis Hamilton, profiled in the chapter Next Generation Boards, evidences another aspect of investing in employee growth through the intensive training and support it provides to the young people that it is opening opportunities for in STEM, motorsport and the creative industries.

Trying to intentionally build or change a culture, even in small organisations, can be hard. In start-ups, the characters of the founders and those of the early hires will be a key determinant of the formative culture. Finding people with the ideal blend of skills, capabilities and character can be tough. Yet many experienced leaders will envy the ability to shape a culture from the start rather than the challenge of changing it. Culture change is not microwaveable. It takes time and once embedded will continue to develop.

Amongst the many characteristics that make up an organisation's culture, our work and research kept gravitating towards five that were integral to maximise the potential of an intergenerational workforce. These were **Collaboration, Respect, Inclusivity, Leadership and Innovation**. Crucially, these are characteristics that can be enhanced without large financial investment or complex processes, and which underpin other common elements of a healthy culture and are central to achieving sustained high performance. These characteristics appeared frequently in our conversations as descriptors of both the people we spoke with, as well as of their organisations and culture.

We have selected a number of examples from our research and conversations to evidence Collaborative, Inclusive and Innovative aspects of culture. All of which are underpinned by demonstrating Respect and Leadership. A simple definition of respect is to show someone consideration – to consider their interests, feelings and ideas and to acknowledge their contribution. Respect underpins collaboration and inclusiveness and is at the core of maximising potential at any age. To enable people from different generations to maximise their potential takes leadership that diverges from this notion of hero leadership, and instead is defined as empowering, energising and collaborative. The word *maximising* is purposeful, as, unless you get lucky, to achieve high performance takes intention and a considerable amount of thought, expertise and motivational capability.

That intention is what we now go on to unpack and demonstrate in opening up a series of cases and conversations, framed through the following chapters: *The Intrapreneurial Mindset, Family Businesses, Next Generation Boards, Intergenerational Alliances* and *Generations Future.*

One of the most striking things for us as we worked on this book was the significance of investing in intrapreneurship, and its role in strengthening a culture of innovation. The cases and conversations that we share in the chapter *The Intrapreneurial Mindset* also embody deep levels of inclusivity. There is no doubt that each of these is driven by the need for these businesses to keep innovating and to be in touch with customers of all generations who buy their products.

Incidentally, one of the most important collaborations in recent times which produced a literally life-saving innovation was the double-layered collaboration of Özlem Türeci, who was 41 when she co-founded BioNTech with 43-year-old Uğur Şahin in 2008. With their company just 12 years old in 2020, the pair then famously collaborated with Pfizer, founded in 1849, to produce one of the main COVID-19 vaccines, demonstrating that intergenerational collaboration can apply to organisations as well as individuals.

In a highly competitive global business, one way of telling whether shareholders really care about fostering collaboration and innovation is through how much hard cash they invest in the business year after year. As we learnt in our interview with André Hoffmann, great-grandson of the founder Fritz Hoffmann, and Vice-Chair, Roche Holdings, in our chapter dedicated to *Family Businesses*, this is a company taking a serious approach to long-term investment: *"When we started the corporate governance and sustainability committee, I said we are going to look at the 100-year plan. Taking a longer-term perspective was relevant for the business that we are in, and it was vitally important for our wider responsibility."*

Next Generation Boards have proven to be another source for stimulating innovation and connecting ideas with an organisation's top decision makers and resource allocators. Amongst a broad spectrum of objectives, they are a means to boost multigenerational collaboration and innovation as well as to increase empathy and understanding across the ages. They also have potential to add considerable value through improving and diversifying the pipeline of talent and skills for board roles. For all these and many other reasons, we have devoted the chapter on *Next Generation Boards* to explore their benefits as well as the practicalities of making them work.

Intergenerational work on large social issues is the focus of *Intergenerational Alliances*, where systems thinking meets sustainable solutions. This chapter shines a light on practical examples and models, from grass-roots work to complex, matrixed organisations. It also engages with companies shifting the needle on age diversity through intergenerational alliances. Age does not seem to have featured as a prominent dimension in diversity and inclusion training, but we suspect this will change. With a view to fuel-inject more senior experience into work, The American Association of Retired Persons (The AARP) are both raising awareness of the importance of creating more age-diverse recruitment processes and developing practical tools for both employers and potential recruits.

Having unpacked the challenges of intergenerational working, and debunked some of the myths, our conversations and case studies took us across continents and cultures, going behind the scenes of work that is moving the multigenerational needle in a series of exciting and progressive ways. We close out with a deeper and wider reflection on *Generations Future*, featuring world-first work. Join us on a journey across cultures, countries and industries that is told through the lenses of five generations. The next chapters and conversations have intentionally been written non-sequentially for you to find the content that interests you most, or that may be most relevant to you.

"Jazz is not a what, it is a how."

Bill Evans

One of the icons of jazz, Bill Evans was one of the most influential pianists of his time, also known for his inimitable improvisation. In this chapter we celebrate companies making space for collaboration and creativity, threading innovation through the organisation.

We celebrate the *how*.

4

The Intrapreneurial Mindset

The influence and impact of 'intrapreneurship' within companies and organisations is often headlined through iconic breakthroughs, such as the Post-it, created within 3M by Spencer Silver and Art Fry, and the PlayStation, envisioned by Ken Kutaragi within Sony. Google's 20% Rule, dedicating 20% of time for employees to work on other projects and pas-

> **"... whereas expertise is the ability to understand something and be in possession of knowledge of information, creativity consists not of having the answers to questions but in asking the right questions."[1]**
>
> Dr. Tomas Chamorro-Premuzic

sions is well known for generating the foundations of key innovations, such as Gmail and AdSense. Intrapreneurship is the practice of fostering entrepreneurial behaviour and initiatives within their organisation, empowering employees to innovate, experiment and develop new ideas or projects. An exploration of the history of intrapreneurship in MIT *Sloan Management Review*[2] tracks one of the earliest manifestations to the 1970s when 'intrapreneurship' was cited by Gifford Pinchot III and Elizabeth Pinchot in their paper "Intra-Corporate Entrepreneurship", and subsequently in their book *Intrapreneuring*.

Gamers and offices, the world over, have Kutaragi, Silver and Fry to thank, with the PlayStation and the Post-it as innovations born of intrapreneurs, but what of intrapreneurial thinking that can address the need for more agile and creative skillsets throughout an organisation? Through the rapidly changing dynamics and forces of technology, climate and the sheer pace of change, how can companies take lessons from intrapreneurial thinking to better enable and empower the skillsets needed to address

61

those changes? Setting the conditions for, and coaching for collaboration, co-creation and connection is becoming ever more fundamental. Our research across generations has led us to explore companies that are seeking to embed a more intrapreneurial mindset and skillset through the organisation, and with opportunities to mobilise talent at scale. We spotlight work that is progressing a mindset and culture of intrapreneurship.

Why does this matter to the multigenerational discourse?

Creativity, collaboration and an agility for learning are amongst the vital and valuable skills that are rising through the age of generative AI. They are skills that transcend – and will, increasingly, need to transcend – disciplines, roles and titles in the workplace. At the same time they are not, necessarily, skills that have been invested in or developed in a multilateral way. Where companies *are* investing in this way, the value of intrapreneurial experiences showed up positively early on in our research. In this chapter we will go on to unpack multicultural, multigenerational and multidisciplinary case studies across different industries and contexts, with lessons that can be applied across companies and organisations of all sizes and scale.

Tolstoy's Bicycle

But first we need to begin with Tolstoy. Or, more specifically, with *Tolstoy's Bicycle*. Lev Tolstoy, author of classics such as *War and Peace* and *Anna Karenina,* learnt to ride a bicycle when he was 67. It was this gem of an anecdote that inspired Jeremy Baker to catalogue 7500 achievements ordered by age, in the book *Tolstoy's Bicycle. Who did what when?* He catalogues achievements in all spheres of life, positing the idea and confirming the point that there is no fixed age for achievement.

As ever, it is the context of Tolstoy and his bicycle that is relevant. Tolstoy was born in 1827. The bicycle did not come into existence until the late 1800s, gaining popularity in the 1880s and 1890s in the US and Europe. So, in 1895, at the age of 67, Tolstoy was in the early wave of bicycle enthusiasts, adopting the new technology when it was available. As we fast forward to the context of our times of generative AI, *Tolstoy's Bicycle* is a mnemonic for debunking the stereotypes. There is no fixed age where curiosity dwindles, or to learn a new way of doing something. And there is no fixed age for achievement.

In our own intergenerational research and the studies that we explored, one stood out in claiming the largest dataset of US entrepreneurs (2.7 million) and examining the relationship between age and entrepreneurial success. It was conducted by Pierre Azoulay, Benjamin F. Jones, J. Daniel Kim and Javier Miranda from Harvard University, studying entrepreneurs from a wide range of sectors.[3] And this is probably the key paragraph from the paper: *"We find no evidence to suggest that founders in their 20s are especially likely to succeed. Rather, all evidence points to founders being especially successful when starting businesses in middle age or beyond. Across the 2.7 million founders in the U.S. between 2007-2014 who started companies that go on to hire at least one employee, the mean age for the entrepreneurs at founding is 41.9. The mean founder age for the 1 in 1,000 highest growth new ventures is 45.0."*

To put this into context, it is worth reminding ourselves of where some of the now most recognised companies, organisations and achievements in the world, began. In the recent decades of tech unicorns and tech giants, the success of founders in their 20s has been well demonstrated and documented with Apple, Microsoft, Meta and Google often cited, all having founders aged from 19 to 25. The origins of more established businesses may not be as fresh in our minds, but they are no less relevant. If we start to look further back, the founders of Bosch, IKEA, Siemens and Sony are amongst a number of leading brands established by founders in their teens or early 20s. What, perhaps, is notably less documented is the entrepreneurship through the other decades of our working lives.

As we look to successful founding stories in their 30s, LinkedIn was founded by Reid Hoffmann at 36, and Netflix by Reed Hastings at 37. One of the most successful movie franchises began in the 38-year-old imagination of Stan Lee, with 'The Fantastic Four', followed by the now iconic characters of the Marvel Universe. The first woman to become a member of the New York Stock Exchange, Muriel Siebert, was 39 when she founded financial services business Siebert, and Cher Wang was on the cusp of her 40th birthday when she founded smartphone business HTC.

The 'forty somethings' also have their entrepreneurial legends, especially in the automotive sector. Henry Ford was 40 when he started the Ford Motor Company, Yoshisuke Aikawa was 48 when he founded Nissan, while Rolls-Royce tells an interesting cross-generational story, founded by Henry Royce, age 43 and Charles Rolls age 29. As we look across other sectors and across centuries, Robin Chase founded ZipCar at 42, the same age as Elisha Otis when he founded Otis in 1853. Eric Yuan created Zoom at 41, the same age at which Christian Dior founded the eponymous luxury brand in the previous century.

Founders in their fifties include Ray Kroc, founder of McDonalds at 52, Henri Nestlé who founded Nestlé at the same age, while Red Bull was created by Chaleo Yoovidhya at 53. At 55, Arianna Huffington founded the Huffington Post, the age at which Coca-Cola was invented by John Pemberton. The Kawasaki motorcycle company was founded by Kawasaki Shozo at 59, and IBM (under its original moniker as the Computer Tabulating Recording Company), was founded by Charles Ranlett Flint at 61. One of our favourite founder stories was that of Garrett Morgan, in 1923, aged 56, inventing what went on to become one of the most universally recognised systems in the world – the three light traffic light.

These stories reinforce two points as we dive into intrapreneurial thinking in action. The first is that the entrepreneurial muscle flexes strong across all ages, which is relevant for how we wire our organisations better for the universally high demand for skills in creativity and innovative thinking. The second is in how we can adapt our hybrid models at work to mutual benefit, with the rise of employees seeking more plural and portfolio careers and driven by the passions of their entrepreneurial side-hustles.

Systemic Intrapreneurship: Building mindset and muscle

Embedding an intrapreneurial mindset can be a powerful way through to build innovation muscle across the business, bringing out the best of generational differences and diversity of lenses. Swiss sports brand On models that very sense of systemic approach. As Chief Marketing Officer Alex Griffin, states: *"It's all about innovation. Every 12-14 months, On becomes a different company. We innovate at such a fast rate because we are trying things that haven't been done before and giving those missions to people which take them out of their comfort zone. We have named On's Headquarters in Zurich 'On Labs' because we encourage innovation to happen everywhere, in all parts of the business."*[4]

Author Nir Bashan (writing in *Psychology Today*) is amongst the advocates of more systemic and integrated approaches to cultures of innovation. An examination of Social Intrapreneur Systems by The World Economic Forum affords a valuable lens here on the value of more systemic approaches for us all, and threading the mindset of intrapreneurship through an organisation:

> *"Intrapreneurs do for organizational innovation what an entrepreneur does for their own start-up, and arguably the case for social intrapreneurship has never been more pressing. Is it enough for discrete products and services to be the output of social intrapreneurs while old cultures and behavioural patterns of organizations remain unchanged?*
>
> *"Social intrapreneurship has had proven success in driving new ideas, products and services – and sometimes even whole new businesses – across industries and contexts. Systemic intrapreneurship could build on that progress, unleashing the true potential of changing systems from within."*[5]

Intrapreneurship may be less documented than entrepreneurship, and manifests in different forms, which is why we want to put the spotlight on a thriving examples of how we can all look to integrate this thinking throughout our companies and organisations. The cases that we explore are also testament to developing the skillsets that will continue to be on the rise, such as agility, creativity and the curiosity for lifelong learning, and reinforce the importance of an age-inclusive approach to innovation as a mindset and skillset.

"Our people are our superpower."

ERICSSON ONE

A platform for intrapreneurs, Ericsson ONE is one of the company's commitments to that celebratory ambition of "Our people are our superpower." They define an intrapreneur as: *"a person who develops new ideas and businesses within a company. They are inventors, pioneers, creators, explorers, doers, and problem-solvers. They have ideas that they believe will make things better or even change the world. They are you."*[6] The intrapreneur model at Ericsson is open to the entire business, across all types of role and all levels of tenure and experience. Salman Taj, VP of Innovation Silicon Valley, Ericsson Business Area Technologies & New Businesses, speaks to inclusive approach and wider value. *"Ericsson One is Ericsson's internal incubator. We have built an organization which supports ALL innovators wishing to disrupt any industry—regardless of previous entrepreneurship experience.*[7] Another defining principle is Ericsson's commitment to only investing in businesses that meet at least one of The UN Sustainable Development Goals.

What is compelling about the approach at Ericsson is how they engage very openly with what is often both 'the elephant in the room' and the barrier for people to get involved, or the blocker preventing these platforms from materialising in the first place – which is the fear of failure. As Daniel Alexus, Head of Ericsson ONE, outlined in an article appositely titled 'Unleashing our Superpower':[8] *"Anyone whose idea is accelerated by Ericsson ONE has the potential to jump from anywhere within Ericsson and become part of the C-Suite of a new venture. And even if an idea fails along the way, the idea owner still would have built new leadership capabilities and experienced accelerated learning that couldn't be replicated in a standard corporate setting. So, even in a failed case, there is massive opportunity for growth."*

Budding intrapreneurs are empowered with a toolkit of resources, from access to the customer base, to sparring with the company-wide pool of talent and technical experts, which in turn opens up new forms of networking across the organisation. And nurturing a spirit of collective creativity and intelligence is something in which the company explicitly seeks to build more muscle through Ericsson ONE's monthly challenges launched through the online platform.

Daniel goes on to articulate the motivations behind some of the innovations, with some that are deeply personal and born from their own experiences, as he outlines in the work pioneered by Parth Radia, Head of Ericsson Digital Human (EDH). *"His motivation to connect with his grandmother, despite the 8,000+ miles between them, led him to create photorealistic holograms and simplified 3D calling. EDH is now the first business from Ericsson ONE to stand alone, and they are continuing to innovate. The EDH team is preparing to roll out an AI-enhanced video API that can translate human video calls both visually and auditorily in real time."*[9]

Rani Yadav-Ranjan, responsible for Technology & Innovation within Ericsson's Global AI Accelerator explains: *"I joined the leadership team of Ericsson's AI Accelerator to address critical business/product problems through technology — which evolved into launching my ideas internally and leading projects that are impacting the organization well beyond my original job description."*[10] The benefits realised are at a number of levels – creating internal mobility pathways for the individual, opportunity for a wider collective, and resulting in impact for the business. As the invitation states at Ericsson ONE: "Engage early and be open to collaboration!"[11]

That openness to collaboration took a different form in another leading global brand that was seeking to channel a generational lens into innovation. That company is hospitality group Accor, who introduced a Shadow Executive Committee. The wider context is key, as the hotels industry was very much in the grips of 'the Airbnb effect' at the time that the Shadow Committee was established, launched in early 2016 by CEO Sébastian Bazin and Chief Talent & Culture officer Arantxa Balson. One of the strategic investments being made by AccorHotels was the creation of a new brand for Millennials. The Accor Shadow Executive Committee, whose members spanned an age range of 25–35 was explicitly hardwired into product and service

❝The ability of these young people to predict the world of tomorrow is finer than ours. In particular on the subjects at the heart of the group's current problems: the expectations of new customers . . . and, more generally, the customer experience.❞[12]

Sébastian Bazin, CEO, Accor Group

innovation. The Millennial Committee acted as an intrapreneurial catalyst within the organisation, connecting into the future of hospitality and the mindset of new generations of customers.

At a time when the hospitality market was being disrupted, this new approach to ideation was a key contributor to Accor's own disruptive solution. And this intrapreneurial, intergenerational investment ultimately resulted in the launch of a new brand in the portfolio – JO&JOE. The Shadow Committee went on to be recognised in the Optimised Business Award at the 2016 Digital Innovation Grand Prix in Paris. What Accor achieved through the leadership's cross-generational strategy, was brand innovation informed and influenced by Millennials, for Millennials.

Multigenerational and multidisciplinary

Intrapreneurial thinking manifests in a powerful way with a pioneering platform that came into being within LVMH in 2017: LVMH DARE!. And to explain why this was so exciting and how it mattered, we need to understand the context of the organisational structure. LVMH is recognised as the leading luxury powerhouse group in the world. The Group encompasses 75 houses, or 'Maisons', across fashion, beauty, watches and jewellery, wines and spirits and wider retail, with fast approaching 200,000 employees worldwide. A family-run business, led by Bernard Arnault, LVMH embeds generational thinking throughout its operations, with the next generations of the Arnault family responsible for some of the most prestigious brand assets. Every member of the Arnault family has a role and responsibility in the business: Delphine Arnault is the CEO of

Christian Dior, Antoine Arnault, Chairman of Loro Piana and head of communications and image at LVMH, Alexandre Arnault, VP Product and Communications of Tiffany, Frédéric Arnault, CEO of LVMH Watches and Jean Arnault, Director of Watches and Marketing at Louis Vuitton.

As we consider the historical timeline of the LVMH portfolio, many of these brands existed long before the generations of today. It is an important factor in how LVMH considers its role as a guardian of these brands – brands that have served customers long before us and that promise to do so long after us. The oldest brand in the portfolio dates from 1365, rooted in the origins of Clos des Lambrays, the oldest wine estate in the LVMH Group, followed by Château d'Yquem in 1593. Beauty brand Buly, established in 1803, and Loewe in 1846, seem young, by comparison.

With such strong verticals in the business, including some of the most valuable brands in the world, in Louis Vuitton and Dior, what was so instructive and constructive about the emergence of the LVMH intrapreneurship platform was the vital horizontal that it effected across Maisons, regions and the respective *savoir-faire* within the Group. As a cross-organisation realisation of the entrepreneurial culture nurtured by Chantal Gaemperle, Group Executive Vice President Human Resources and Synergies, it tapped into a need to amplify mindset and skillset

> **"Our model, which is based on a long-term vision, values the heritage of our Houses and stimulates creativity and excellence. It is the driving force for the Group's success and the guarantee of its future."**
>
> Bernard Arnault

in the commitment to creativity and excellence, which is at the core of the Group.

Operating across a multigenerational and multidisciplinary framework, DARE is a catalyst for transformative thinking, a central crucible of knowledge and ideas, and a connector of people through and across the organisation. The platform exercises muscle in both collaboration and in collective intelligence – from bonding and binding people who have never met in the organisation through shared work on projects and prototypes, to a living body of insight and ideas that can be drawn on from every Maison.

DARE – Disrupt, Act, Risk to be an Entrepreneur! – is the call to action of The DARE programme and platform, which is live throughout the year for talents to propose innovative ideas, to connect and collaborate. Participants are supported by mentors – including CEOs from LVMH Maisons and external entrepreneurs – to help them refine their business model, to test their prototype and prepare their final pitch. The intrapreneur participants are invited to pitch their project to a jury composed of LVMH top executives and external experts or entrepreneurs. The programme has already supported the launch and acceleration of over 52 innovative projects. With thousands of ideas on display across all business categories, the platform is also a unique opportunity for Maisons to leverage collective intelligence across the Group.

And, of course, the big question was, how did this all begin? And that, as we go on to unpack in a conversation with Laetitia Roche-Grenet, Director of LVMH Open Innovation, was a story of intrapreneurship in itself.

LVMH DARE

Dare to DARE!

Paris

> *"The generational exchange
> is very important"*

LVMH DARE began with the combined ambition and insight of one individual, who was managing a brand in the LVMH Group. That ambition was born out of a curiosity and motivation to achieve more within the organisation. It was 2016 – and there was a pivot in the making. I had the privilege to go back to the beginning and behind the scenes with the person behind that pivot – **Laetitia Roche-Grenet, architect of LVMH DARE and Director of Open Innovation at LVMH.**

Laetitia, how did it all begin?

I was the General Manager of Fred, one of the jewellery brands in the LVMH portfolio, where I had had a wonderful career trajectory for four years. And I had reached a point where I wanted to do something else. Fred was one of many brands in the group, and I really didn't know a lot about the other brands of the group. When you are part of a brand, you are very focused on that brand, and you don't have a real vision across the other brands that are part of LVMH. That was really the first insight, as I wanted and needed to learn more about what was happening in the group to understand where I could project my next chapter.

As I was starting to reach out to people, I got a phone call one day from Pascal Jouvin (who runs LVMH House and programmes for high potential development and top management). He spoke with me about the importance of the entrepreneurial spirit for LVMH and its brands, and how we needed to do more to cultivate it. As the Maisons are very independent, there really was work to be done in creating some links.

And that was the first spark for me. That same evening, I started writing a job description.

The following week, I started the journey to what you see today. The first step was to create a connection between the autonomous Maisons. I invented the first event with design thinking – it was the first time in the story of LVMH that Chantal Gaemperle, Group Executive Vice President Human Resources and Synergies, sent a call for ideas to all the Maisons. That was a really powerful moment at a cultural level of the organisation, and a first in the group and in the Maisons for that type of communication. And we received hundreds of ideas! Of course, the big question was how do we select them? We invited senior executives from the Maisons to get involved, and some of the projects from that first year went on to become a reality for the Group.

And fast-forward to today – how does DARE manifest now?

Today, we have expanded the ecosystem both internally within the LVMH Group, as well as externally. We now have the DARE Games across the entire Group, which is a regional competition. We currently have 30,000 people on the platform, and the DARE Games has received the maximum number of ideas in the history of the programme.

In parallel we opened in Station F in Paris, known as the world's biggest start-up campus – because it's external, and it's where we accelerate business solutions with the Maisons. In 2016 I was one person doing this for two years – without a budget or a team. Now we are a team where we are a central force for innovation, listening to the needs of the Maisons, sourcing the right solutions, incubating and accelerating them. And we have a strong mantra of openness – and showcasing what we do. VivaTech, the annual global conference dedicated to innovation, is important for us both externally, and internally, where the Maisons can really see and experience what we do. We have now become a department of open innovation.

What were the success factors and lessons that you would pass on to others?

DARE brings together the hierarchies of the organisation, across the most junior and senior employees. This has been a highly successful part of it. It also works because we don't 'over-KPI'[13] it – we created an open platform, set some big ambitions, and the rest is for the individuals and the teams to make it happen. There are new skills that they might need to learn, or to put to the test – such as who they find to sponsor them to make their solution a reality. And we keep it moving – DARE Games is a new format that we introduced on a regional level, so thinking about the ways in which we constantly keep it relevant. And we will continue to evolve it. The generational exchange is very important – people in the teams are working across generations and disciplines – and the more diverse the teams, the better.

One of the biggest results that we could never have predicted was what DARE did for us through COVID and lockdown – the platform remained one of our constants and was always on. We had built a destination that became a community. Over that time many more people joined the platform. We were hosting big talks discussing solutions to the COVID, we hosted the first global webinar in LVMH with thousands of our employees connected. Going back to what we experienced as a result of DARE during the pandemic – so many times in companies, we hear people talk about the 'nice to haves', and this really became a 'must have'.

I believe in organic movement. And what I love is that it has brought generations together. Our people have not only the potential, but now the platform to change the future of the LVMH Group. People are motivated to join for different reasons – sometimes it is to discover more about the Group, for some it is about finding their way in their next career, for others it is about launching a project – the common theme is they can all change something, together, for the future of the Group. Nona Source is a great example of a progressive company born out of the programme. A high-end materials resale platform, taking deadstock fabrics and leather from the world's leading fashion Maisons under the LVMH umbrella, it supports one of the ambitions of the LVMH environmental strategy to foster greater creative circularity in the fashion industry. Importantly, Nona Source was not about being the most radical or unique idea – what was successful was that it had relevance and value for all the Maisons.

And as we close out the conversation, Laetitia imparts a trinity of lessons: "Anybody can inspire us. It is about staying humble – and listening. Something very small today can become something huge tomorrow."

FAST FACTS

LVMH DARE

Platform:	Intrapreneur platform, programme and ecosystem
Geography:	Global
Industries:	Fashion; Food and beverage; Lifestyle; Jewellery; Luxury
Launched:	2017
Purpose:	LVMH DARE encourages all talents to share bold ideas, to connect and collaborate
Composition:	Company-wide
Sponsor:	Laetitia Roche-Grenet

"...meaning that secures our difference, our human difference."

Toni Morrison

Recognised for works of "visionary force and poetic import", Tony Morrison was the first African American to be awarded in Nobel history. These words were written in her soul-stirring acceptance speech for the Nobel Prize for literature.

In this chapter, we explore the human difference and generational lessons at the heart of some of the world's family businesses.

5

Family Businesses

Through a succession of leadership across 46 generations, the Hokuriku Awazu Onsen Hoshi is one of the oldest family businesses in Japan, dating back to the year 718 AD, and continues to thrive today.[1] Similarly, the success of Nishiyama Onsen Keiunkan, founded in 705, is cited for its "intergenerational pride".[2]

The intergenerational dimension to family businesses made it integral to our work and to this discussion, as we were curious to go deeper into some of the drivers behind the models of success and sustainability. The other factor behind their relevance is the sheer scale of their influence and impact on the global economy. Two-thirds of companies globally are family-owned, generating 70% of the world's GDP. As the Global Family Business Index, published by EY and the University of St Gallen evidences, the largest 500 family businesses are growing faster than the global economy, collectively generating US $8.02 trillion in revenues and employing 24.5 million people worldwide.[3]

Having gained insight and sightlines from our own experience and work with family businesses, we explore in more depth how positive aspects of their cultures could be adopted and adapted to boost the cultures and performance of non-family organisations. Through the course of our research, we examined how they integrate generational thinking into the operationalisation of the business, the structuring of family and non-family roles and responsibilities, succession planning and business evolution and innovation. Importantly, there is an inherent sense of guardianship of a company or organisation that takes on a different level of meaning in sustaining a business inspired by one founding generation for future generations.

What can we learn from family businesses?

Family businesses are in unique positions when it comes to defining decisions for the long term, from investment in the business to succession. At the same time, they face challenges that do not exist in the same way in public companies, including managing the dynamics of family members, and the emotional conflict that can go along with it. They are a rich source of insights in the context of the multigenerational workplace, because of the diversity in their dimensions:

- Family businesses operate under a range of ownership structures, as public or private companies, with or without other shareholders, which create different dynamics. The structure is such that they can have other major shareholders, while some are public companies. VW is an example of a public company controlled by family through voting rights rather than shareholding.
- They have different leadership and operational structures, in terms of control over decision-making, board and leadership team involvement and multiple generations working in the business.
- The family means of influence, beyond ownership and leadership also varies, including the name of the business, involvement in decision-making and the influence that the family has over the culture and the organisation.

- They have a vested interest in the multigenerational make-up – some are intentionally multigenerational, others become more intentional over time. Time is an operative word for many family businesses, who tend to have a longer-term perspective.

Through the course of this chapter and in our conversations, we explore and unpack:

The stewardship mindset and investing for the long term. This taps into the good ancestor principle that we hear in multiple conversations and that reverberates in other chapters.

A sense of purpose and shared value. This is about the importance of their driving purpose in contributing to sustained success, and the role that family businesses play in the communities and societies where they operate – two aspects that make them different. This connection to the founding purpose shines through in the case of Mars as we go on to explore in this chapter, remaining deeply relevant to the business of today. And there are lessons for all businesses from the counterpoint, where that purpose may be less defined, or may go unchronicled, and lose relevance over time.

The opportunity and freedom to innovate. Looking at how philosophies of long-term innovation are realised, including creating the space and providing the resources, and how adjacent generations are bridging the dynamic of tradition and innovation to sustain relevance.

Succession planning and sustainability of the family business. The regeneration and evolution of leadership

> **"Good governance is about vision into the future. A family business is a platform – and it's how you utilise that platform to drive success through the business – and for others."**
>
> Lauri Oinaala, EMEIA Family Enterprise Leader, EY

involving both family members and those who are "adopted" into the family firm, which aligns the most relevant leadership with the context and phase of development of the business.

As a stewardship mindset and investing for the long-term frame the other dimensions, also providing the motivation to achieve them successfully, this seems a logical place to start.

Stewardship mindset and investing for the long term

Stewardship as a mindset means taking care of something during our time and leaving it in a good state for our successors. It requires a lens on the long term. As Lauri Oinaala emphasises, the strongest family businesses are platforms that enable the realisation of that vision into the future. Dedicated to representing and supporting family businesses to create a more sustainable future for generations to come, Family Business UK (FBUK) is the largest organisation in the UK, whose community stretches across some of the largest and oldest British businesses, as well as first-generation businesses.

Neil Davy, CEO of FBUK reinforces that wider sense of how purpose runs through all the generational pieces, from senior gen to next gen. *"There are very different motives with family businesses. The ownership model is based on different motives, in how they are run and the importance of relationships and values. We ask the question – is the purpose of the business to maximise profit, or is the profit an outcome of a business well managed? Family businesses tend to have this ethos of profit as an outcome of a business well managed because they are thinking about the next gen. The important point here in the intergenerational piece is why family businesses matter, and how this matters to their very purpose and existence. In that context it's not divisive from a generational perspective. Every generational change is a shift in priorities when the rising gen of family businesses become the next custodian. It's about creating an environment for those stakeholders to come together."*

Throughout our research and work with family businesses, and in the cases and conversations in this chapter, stewardship is a perennial red thread. Family businesses were some of the early movers in stakeholder capitalism, as we explore in our conversations with Ahlström, founded in 1851 and Mars, founded in 1911. Long-term commitments to regeneration resonate in our conversations with both Hoffmann-La Roche and The Pentland Group. For Finnish industrial pioneer Ahlström, as we learn from family member Maria Ahlström-Bondestam: "doing the right thing by their community and society was doing right by their business, and it was part of what enabled it to thrive". The company was one of the pioneers in the prominence of women in business with Antti's wife Eva going on to become one of the first female Finnish industrialists.

A sense of purpose & shared value

In 2018, a *Harvard Business Review* study of the UK's longest-lasting organisations found that those that stand the test of time focus not just on "serving customers, owning resources, being efficient and growing", but also "try to shape society, share experts . . . and focus on getting better not bigger".[4] Generativity is something that James H. Davis talks about in *"the motivation to build legacy generativity, and it stems from the concern for the welfare, well-being and security of future generations. This desire has been found to exist more in family firms than non-family firms because of an increased feeling of moral obligation to past and future generations."*[5]

Lauri Oinaala, EMEIA Family Enterprise Leader at EY talks about the wider context of the transfer of ownership and the role of the next generations in this unprecedented time of transition: *"As family businesses around the world go through the greatest generational transition in history, the new generation of owners are transforming their businesses through this rapid pace of change, disruption of industries and wider societal responsibility. There are three things that are true of extremely successful families – they ensure that all stakeholders are well considered, they combine a strong stewardship mentality with an entrepreneurial culture, and they are making sustained commitments to societal impact. What's especially important with next generations is how ownership enables the business to commit to and work on matters that deliver for the broader society. Good governance is about vision into the future. A family business is a platform – and it's how you utilise that platform to drive success through the business – and for others."*

As reported by Forbes India, in a series dedicated to the next-gen evolution of family businesses, the common ingredient to the success of the models is 'values'. *"What has remained constant with most family businesses is the core value system"* states Aakanksha Gandhi, fourth generation of Vadilal, one of the most recognised ice-cream brands in India, and who is responsible for marketing and branding nationwide. As she enthuses: *"Being in a generational family business, there is always an opportunity to add value to the legacy. Since becoming part of the brand, my primary goal has been to ensure continued relevance among the Gen Z and Gen Alpha demographics."*[6]

Values run deep in the family businesses that we explore in this chapter. What is striking is how resonant they are in conversations with both family and non-family members, and in the role that they play as central organising principles of the business. As Andrew Stanley, CISO & VP Global Digital Operations, Mars says: *"I've always connected with this idea that we all have a vested interest in each other. It is incredibly human. It's very explicit here."*[7]

The opportunity and freedom to innovate

Japan is home to some of the oldest family businesses in the world, whose continuity today is the result of how they carry forward their unique knowledge and expertise from one generation to the next. Established in 1688 in Kyoto, leading textile brand Hosoo is world renowned for its excellence in the manufacture and craftsmanship of silk. One of the drivers behind this sustained success is their ability to carry forward their time-honoured tradition, while constantly evolving and innovating. That commitment to innovation is thriving in Hosoo Studios, its R&D division, which collaborates on textile innovation with an ecosystem of other brands, and universities. This is a vital catalyst to enabling Hosoo's work to reach new audiences through creative collaborations with brands, such as Gucci and The Four Seasons, and through key partnerships, such as LVMH Métiers d'Art.

This constant evolution between tradition and innovation as intrinsic to a brand's intergenerational appeal is something that Hiroyui Murase speaks to: "*. . . it's the fact that techniques from 400 years ago can create innovation — that is really attractive to the new generation. Thanks to those collaborations, they see a new side to the craft.*"[8] Murase is the founder of luxury brand Suzusan, which is a spin-off of his family's fifth-generation business.

Succession

"*Succession works most effectively when it's looked at as a multistakeholder activity*" continues FBUK's Neil Davy. "*Family businesses are culturally worlds apart because there is an openness, a willingness to support, a desire to share and learn. Language speaks volumes when you speak with family businesses. One of the indicators is the businesses who 'communicate with'. They are constantly listening. As a result, one of the things that many do very well is the collaboration between senior gen and now gen around how they can best create an environment for the next gen to carry forward the business. They are thinking about a diversity of pathways into the family business and how the two meet each other. Equally, within our next gen community, there are conversations on how they can share their views upwards—and how you do it in a way that doesn't suggest entitlement."*

Another insight into where other businesses and organisations might take inspiration from family businesses is in how senior gen experience is valued, and in their approach to knowledge transfer. As Fiona Graham, Director of External Affairs and Policy at FBUK, says: *"One of the challenges for family businesses is what that senior family member's role looks like, how it evolves, and how the role might shift to become more philanthropic at this point in time. In the context and impact of longer lifetimes, it's thinking progressively around making space for the next generation, with senior gen providing counsel and wisdom. There are lessons here in how family businesses invest in knowledge transfer and in how they value experience and expertise."* In our conversations with Mars and The Pentland Group, this investment in succession is an integral part of the strategy and evidenced in a range of intentional intergenerational work within their businesses.

Our conversations and research into the insights and lessons from the multigenerational thinking, operations and philanthropy of family businesses took us across Asia, Europe and the Americas, including some of the oldest family businesses in the world, speaking with generations of family members and serving board members. In this chapter, we unpack the intergenerational dynamics of four family businesses. Finnish industrialist **Ahlström** share with us how, in such a large family, with 420 family members, they succeed in marrying their values with structure. The lessons for us all are in how collaborative leadership works to the good of collective impact. We gain deep insight from a business taking a 100-year view, with **Hoffmann-La Roche,** where investment in innovation is core to the business, and where family member André Hoffmann is an advocate for family businesses as models for intergenerational equity and regenerative thinking.

The family business behind many of the most recognised confectionery brands in the world, with one of the largest petcare portfolios, **Mars** is a powerful example of a very private family business, operating at scale. We explore the Mars Compass and the importance of the guiding principles by which the business lives, operates and innovates. As Andrew Clarke, Mars Snacking Global President states: *"I think in generations, not quarters. We can do things for the long-run, we can innovate for the long-run. We can build for the long-run."*[9] **The Pentland Group** is a fourth-generation business, operating a group of winning brands in sports and lifestyle. We gain a powerful perspective on the responsibility of ownership and how the family has integrated intergenerational thinking into the fabric of the Group.

AHLSTRÖM

Collective impact

Helsinki, Finland

Ahlström is one of the most significant industrial families in Finland, founded by industrialist Antti Ahlström. The company was one of the pioneers in the prominence of women in business with Antti's wife Eva going on to become one of the first female Finnish industrialists. Dating from the 1850s, Ahlström has grown from its origins in shipping to become a strategic owner investing in companies in industry, real estate and forestry across the world.

We spoke with **Maria Ahlström-Bondestam, fifth-generation family member, Member of the Supervisory Board and Nominations Committee, and Co-founder and Honorary Chair of the Eva Ahlström Foundation, which was inspired by her great-great-grandmother.**

The foundations of the family business are truly game-changing, in this early commitment to equality and to the wider contribution to society. How does this resonate today?

The older I get, the prouder I am of my heritage and ancestors. As a man, Antti was a feminist who championed women's rights and who helped to change the law which enabled women to inherit. This is why the women in our family now own 50% of the company. In many families it would be the eldest male, but from the start it was equal.

We are a very big family – with 7 generations and 420 members in the family. Of those members, roughly half are shareholders. And we calculate family as everyone who is born and married into it. Therefore we differ somewhat from other families in how we look at family members, but it goes back to this founding belief in equality. And perhaps there is also the cultural context of coming from a small country, where we believe in the importance of educating and including everyone. We can't afford to exclude people.

What was vital to the success of Antti and Eva from the very beginning was their understanding of the importance of investing in society. Doing the right thing by their community and society was doing right by their business and it was part of what enabled it to thrive. And it sets the wider scene for how Finland evolved, and how our business played a role in that evolution, along with other family businesses. How we look at prosperity and interdependence created a success story for Finland and how equality thrives today. And as a family we really feel this sense of generational pride. This respect for each other, this sense of what you believe in and how you create wealth over time all comes down to your values.

> *"It's about a more collaborative leadership, creating the space and support structure for people to be their best in their role."*

What is the role of the family in the business today, and how is the board constructed?

Since the previous generation, the family has not been operationally active, but has held Board and other positions of trust within the family and company sphere (such as the Nomination Committee and Supervisory Board). This has been a purposeful decision that came from the generation before us to instil skills and best practice from outside the family and to ensure that we elected the most qualified person for each position. At the time this was the right thing to do – but what we found after one generation was it then started to lose contact to the values and will of the family and a sense of who we are. Today we have nine family members on the Supervisory Board, of which four are from the next generation, and three external members. And it's important to say that the election process for Board positions is the same as for external candidates. Today, for the first time since the matriarch Eva Ahlström, the Chair of the Supervisory Board is a female family member. The Chair of our business operations is a male family member joined by six family members working operationally in the company. Our family member representation is also multigenerational across both fifth and sixth generations.

Today we have more of a sense of who we are, we feel our DNA. As the family is involved again with greater influence, we have been working on our values, which are ambition and responsibility – the ambition to be the best version of yourself, and the responsibility as a shareholder and citizen. And these values play an active role in what we do. We hold ourselves accountable by our values, and we call each other out on our values.

Another important element of cohesion is trust, and how we create trust in each other. As a large family, it's why we create space for us to connect, and our philanthropy work plays a part in that bonding and binding. It's about a more collaborative leadership, creating the space and support structure for people to be their best in their role.

In your strategic plan, one of the things that you talk about as fundamental to the whole business is being a "Custodian of family heritage assets".

I feel it is such an honour and a privilege to be able to contribute to society, to have the possibility to effect change. I have actively been involved in the family business for 15 years, and I believe you need to inspire, engage and include everyone. You need to give everyone a possibility to contribute, and in a big family that's making sure that everyone feels that they are part of this greater whole. This is part of my own sense of my heritage and place in society, and I made it my mission to do this in the family, to make sure that everyone knows that they matter and how their respective skills matter, and that when we combine all our strengths as a family, we have the power to effect change.

I have also noticed a change in how my own skillset is seen over the past 15 years. I like to think that I have been an empathetic leader. And, when we look back, words like 'empathy' were hardly talked about in business 15 years ago, but now empathy has become part of the biggest currency. Language has changed. Language has reflected the change.

Is there a wider context here that comes into play of Nordic boards, leadership and governance?

In the Nordics it's in our DNA that we are all equal and deserve a fair chance in life. So in that sense it's easier than in some markets and cultures. The mindset makes it easier.

Philanthropy plays an important role in your family, from the Foundation that you co-founded, to the Ahlström Collective Impact platform, which unites public and private companies, foundations, shareholders and employees in partnership with UNICEF Finland to support the realisation of The UN Sustainable Development Goals (SDGs).

Philanthropy plays a very important part. We have the Eva Ahlström Foundation that I established with my 25 female cousins, which supports vulnerable women and children. Collective Impact came about as we looked at what we could do within our company and wider network. It is a collaborative platform than enables everyone in the Ahlström network, all our companies, our 15,000 employees across the world and our shareholders, to participate. Almost all of the companies are members of Collective Impact, with one person from every company serving on the Steering Committee. That board is also multigenerational. The mission is to give everyone the possibility to contribute to the realisation of the SDGs. And for that to happen I believe everyone needs to understand *what* rights children have and *how and why* their realisation affects our businesses, societies and joint future. Change will happen when people change. A good heart and intentions are important, but change will happen only when you *act* on your values, intentions and good heart. As owners this is our will. It is our conviction and determination to live and build upon these values first established by Antti and Eva. This is about the type of companies that we want to pass on to our children.

HOFFMANN-LA ROCHE

The 100-year view
Sustainable, inclusive prosperity

Geneva, Switzerland

The Hoffmann name will be widely recognised from the name of leading healthcare company Hoffmann-La Roche. What might be less well known is the fact that it is one of the oldest privately held family businesses in the world. Founded in 1896 by entrepreneur Fritz Hoffmann, the company has evolved through five generations. We spoke with **André Hoffmann, great-grandson of the founder Fritz Hoffmann, and Vice-Chair, Roche Holdings.**

André, there are a number of points of shared value through our respective work across generations. Could we open by giving everyone a lens on the family business today?

My great-grandfather created the company. And through the course of the history of Hoffmann-La Roche, it was felt that it would be better for the company if the family did not have an active management role in the business. Since the 1930s, we have not been that active in the management role of the company, but the family concentrated on governance through active participation on the board. We have two board members – a role that traditionally is handed over through members from either side of the family. I was elected 27 years ago. My nephew is fifth generation and is a member of the audit committee.

What was the logic of no active management?

Fortune magazine published an article in the 1970s featuring a small family business in Switzerland that had become the biggest pharmaceutical company on the planet. That company was ours. And it painted a picture of my grandfather as a conductor, which was his profession, but not as an active owner representative. And that was a very interesting metaphor to reflect on.

When I was elected, I realised that there was a set of stakeholders that I needed to think deeply about: the family, the management and the other owners. The experience now, 27 years later, is that the management are completely at ease. What was, perhaps, more of a revelation for me, was that I had to address the family as whole. We were eight people in total, and we still are – we are not a huge family – but to bring everyone all together, to have a collective thinking was difficult. What helped during that process was when one of our competitors – Novartis – tried to acquire us. We would have become the largest pharmaceutical company in the world at that time – born out of two companies based in Switzerland. But we also have a saying: 'The bread is always better in the village with two bakers'. Needless to say, we didn't merge. The important point from that story is that sometimes the challenge and threat of external forces can help you – and that moment helped us unify, and we retained our independence.

We have a voting agreement, but not an ownership agreement, and where every generation has the opportunity to renegotiate the agreement. We have a family council that meets regularly, and through this we decide what is voted at the AGM. Board composition is where we spend the most time.

What are the biggest challenges?

When we started the corporate governance and sustainability committee, I said we are going to look at the 100-year plan. Taking a longer-term perspective was relevant for the business that we are in, and it was vitally important for our wider responsibility. We define ourselves as an innovation company, and the company has been reinvented several times in the service of innovation.

We started merging much more of the work that I was doing on nature conservation within the company. We talked about next generations in the context of how we run the business – beyond short-term profit to value for the long-term. For example, we just inaugurated a discovery accelerator in Shanghai, and the cost of that is evident, but this is about investing in future generations. As a business, we see our consumers and patients as stakeholders, and we want to ensure that they get the benefit of long-term thinking. We are united on this cultural issue.

"As an owner, I like to think in 100-year timescales. That sounds incredibly long. But that's the sort of timescale we need."

And that culture of innovation and intrapreneurship – how do you stimulate that?

Our research scientists are the heroes of the company. We tried to become more agile, and we want to attract that agility. We reinvest 20% of our turnover in R&D, and that turnover may not yield an immediate return, but it will for the next generation.

Succession is an important part of these 100-year timescales. When you think about your own succession, how will you organise and think about that?

That's a good one – I would like to believe that as a family we are principle based, not rule based. We would like to defend the same ideals – this long-term thinking. There are three things to do as owners: 1. Understand how we can manage impact – and measure impact, on social, human and economic capital. This is the whole area of business as a force for good – to move from extraction to regeneration; 2. We need to put a price on nature, and nature-based solutions; and 3. We need to develop the people who are going to do it, their capabilities, and the ability to manage conflict through it – and that needs courage, humility, boldness. It's creating a philosophy.

As part of your work across the Weidenfeld-Hoffmann Trust and the World Economic Forum, you talk about "shifting from the many dissonances of today to "*collective creativity*". "*That ambitious goal cannot*

be achieved without engaging with humility in mutual learning across generations. We do not have the right responses to transmit to younger and future generations; more than ever, our exploratory task has to be done together with them." Could you talk with us more about all of this . . . ?

I am a member of The Club of Rome, who had written this model 50 years ago about the limits to growth. When you plug into this scenario, you realise it's a question of inequalities, and the tensions on the system. That should give us some pause to think – and how important it is to move from this historic model of domination to a model of collaboration. We need to work together to a solution. We need to think more about private–public partnerships.

Some cultures talk about seven-generation thinking. When you take a decision, you are thinking very seriously about the long-term impact of that decision. I think about the people who built the great cathedrals that they never saw finished, and that we enjoy and appreciate today thanks to their vision and thinking.

And one last thing. Our jobs, all of us individually, are to work towards sustainable, inclusive prosperity. Or we will not have a future. We need to collectively use our capability and possibility to do that, and by investing in a sustainable way, in a nature-positive way, emboldening people to take on this vision and brave view of the world.

MARS

The power of principles

McLean, Virginia

A family business that thinks in generations, Mars was started with Frank Mars making butter cream candies in his kitchen in 1911. Known today for brands, such as M&M's, Snickers, Royal Canin, VCA and Pedigree, it has since gone on to become a leading business in confectionery, food and petcare products and services, employing 150,000 Associates in 80 countries around the world. What may be less known about Mars is that it was one of the early pioneers of stakeholder capitalism. There is, perhaps, no better place to begin than with a letter – written by Frank in 1947:

THE COMPANY'S OBJECTIVE

The company's objective is the manufacture and distribution of food products in such manner as to promote a mutuality of service and benefits among:

CONSUMERS

DISTRIBUTORS

COMPETITORS

OUR DIRECT SUPPLIERS OF GOODS AND SERVICES

GOVERNMENTAL BODIES

ALL EMPLOYEES OF THE COMPANY

AND

ITS SHAREHOLDERS

This expresses the total purpose for which the Company exists – nothing less – and it is expected that the Board of Directors, all Management and employees of the Company, will be motivated by this basic objective, and will keep it constantly in mind as the guiding principle in all their work for the Company.

28th July 1947
FHS/nc.

The purpose of the company was to deliver a mutuality of service and benefits to a range of groups, including employees, partners, owners and even competitors. That approach remains the North Star of Mars today, guided by its Principles, which play an extraordinary role in the business. *"As a global company with the footprint of a small country, we have the responsibility – and the opportunity – to leave a lasting impact on the world. As a family-owned business, we have the ability to think in generations, rather than just business quarters and have our **Purpose** to guide us on our way."*

"The world we want tomorrow starts with how we do business today" is how Mars defines its Purpose today. Quality, Responsibility, Mutuality, Efficiency and Freedom are the uniting Principles across geographies, cultures and generations. The importance of the Principles resonates in everything that they do: *"Together, they serve as a guide that every Associate can depend on to make decisions – big or small – knowing that when we look at a problem through the collective lens of the Five Principles, we will reach a stronger decision. They are at the heart of the success we've enjoyed over the decades and will continue to guide us in the decades to come."*

We spoke with **Mars family members Frank Mars, Stephen Badger and Victoria Mars, all current or former Board members, who have all spent time as Chair of the Mars Board. We also spoke with non-family members Andy Pharoah, Vice-President of Corporate Affairs and Sustainability, and former Mars Associate Fiona Dawson, CBE, who had a 30-year career at Mars, before retiring from the business in 2021 as Global President of Mars Food, Drinks, Multisales and Global Customers.** Importantly, having held each conversation individually, gaining a diversity of lenses on the family business, what was particularly striking in reflecting on the totality of those experiences and perspectives, was the shared language. Asking the same questions of everyone, we have threaded the answers to convey a sense of the 'red thread' that we experienced from one conversation to another.

As fourth-generation family members, your roles and experience through the evolution of the business are all very different. Could you share your trajectories and stories with us?

Victoria: "As family businesses grow, they learn to do things differently. No two family members are the same. I did things differently from others in my generation of the family, spending my whole career at Mars, beginning in marketing as a brand manager in France. My father and uncle had instilled in us all the concept that you start at the bottom. Just because we were going to be an owner did not entitle us to start at the top of the company. During the summers, we all worked in all aspects of the business, from working in the factories packing the candy to mixing gravy. After university, I started out as a junior brand manager in France and worked my way through different jobs and opportunities. I had some mentoring from some of the more experienced managers, but there was no special treatment. Eventually I came back to the US to get an MBA from Wharton in finance, which gave me different opportunities in the US. It all culminated in me matching my passions with what I'm good at – which is around people."

Stephen: "There are many pathways that lead us through life. Originally I didn't want to work for a large corporate and thought about a family business in a burdensome way. I then came across an organics business called Seeds of Change, and it made me think about how business and social conscience could come together. I went on to sell it into Mars, under the auspices of that, taking the family business into organic food. And it totally transformed the way I thought about Mars. It was the first big moment when I came to see that the Five Principles were really valuable and central to how we operate. In due course and many years after running this relatively small business, through which I learned a lot about business in general and Mars specifically, I went on to run Corporate Affairs globally, then onto the board where I have done two rotations as Chair."

Frank: "I have been in the business for 33 years, starting out working for my grand-dad which was fascinating. I learned a lot. After business school and getting my MBA, I ran my own business before moving on to work for Mars. In Europe I ran the manufacturing supply for food and pet, then snack, and from there worked out of Asia. While there, my father and uncle asked if I would be willing to develop a life science venture in the business. There are things that Mars had been investing in, such as canine

DNA and cocoa science – cocoa science we've since taken to a whole other level, working with universities in the UK and effectively qualifying it as an essential nutrient for health, and with new standards coming in. We have also now established a whole venturing concept – Sustainable Solutions – where we are developing scalable solutions to increase the sustainability of key supply ecosystems and business and ecosystem preservation. I was Chairman of the Board since the start of COVID-19, handing over last year (2023) to one of my cousins and am now back into problem solving and working on special projects as a Mars Associate."

> **"One of the great myths of family businesses as a generic is that it's easy – it's the obverse. You are there with the people whose money it is."**
>
> Fiona Dawson, CBE

The Five Principles are referenced consistently in every conversation, both within and outside the business. It's clear that they are key in connecting culture to collaborative and competitive advantage. How have they come to play such a special role, and what do they mean to you?

Andy: "The Five Principles that the business lives by are firmly wedded to a constant commitment to its good stewardship, its evolution of the business and to how it values all generations across the global business. **'Quality, Responsibility, Mutuality, Efficiency, and Freedom'** have been in place as codified principles for over 40 years. But they all hark back to the way of running Mars that was set out in the 1947 letter, offering a link with our traditions and a bridge to the future."

Victoria: "Our Principles are the family's values, which came from my grandfather and the third generation. As they were created by the family, they are owned by the family, and any changes have to come through the family. Importantly, we have embedded them into the whole organisation, including acquired businesses, because these Principles are non-negotiable. The newest relaunch of the Five Principles was a work of love, process and refresh, to reflect the business that we are today and the current generation. Our culture comes from these Five Principles – how we treat people and value all Associates regardless of hierarchy. This is beyond words on the wall, as it can be in some businesses. Everyone is expected to live the Five Principles when making decisions, from how we hire, to how we promote."

Stephen: "The principles are the throughline in the business for me – they bring us together as a family and as Associates. There is a united agreement around their value in how the business is run and in how we envision the future of the business."

Victoria: "You can see the power of those Principles when you are using them in new contexts. When I was Chair, I had a lot of interactions with senior government people, building trust and relationships – the Principles were my go-to because I could always pull them out when I was having a discussion about how we operate our business. And they inform so much, from opportunity to risk – they are defining the value exchange."

Language clearly matters at Mars. The language that businesses choose to express what matters and how it makes

a difference is always telling. We find the Principles of Freedom and Mutuality particularly compelling.

Victoria: "Mutuality and Freedom are unique. It comes back to our way of looking at the world – Mutuality is a win-win relationship – with all our stakeholders, including consumers and suppliers. Together we will be stronger. We are both getting a benefit. That really came from my grandfather – it's been there from the beginning. The Freedom principle is about our freedom as a business to have control over our own destiny. To be free to make the right decisions. What makes Mars culture is the combination of all five. It's not ok to say I live one principle – I need to live all five."

Fiona: "I was at Mars for over 30 years, and worked with fourth-generation family members, John, Forrest Jr and Jacquie. When I think about the Principles, "mutuality" always stood out as something special. It's not something that you see or hear in many other companies – it is also about mutual accountability. The premise is that shared benefit is an enduring benefit. Quality is another principle that has a much further reach beyond quality of product – quality of growth was a really important consideration, determining which categories and geographies we decided to be in, or not."

Frank: "I would argue that it's Mutuality, Freedom and Responsibility that are different for us. Mutuality is the most important as a tool for good – shared benefit will endure. But it is still massively misunderstood in industry, which has been led by the opposite of mutuality, so it can be a challenge in the boardroom and in operations when you're making longer-term decisions. Looking at the Five Principles through a lens of how to run the business, Mutuality sits in the middle. We have Quality and Efficiency, as the corporate and global perspective on the one side of the spectrum. On the other end, we have Freedom and Responsibility – which is important for local businesses to be in touch with their consumers and the freedom to take decisions. As new Presidents take over, it's finding that balance. Key to that is this concept of ownership, where we encourage people to take a decision, rather than make a decision. Taking a decision is about the Principle of Responsibility. It's that ownership mindset."

"We talk a lot about language because it can make a difference. Procurement for us sits within Commercial because it's about *sourcing* vs buying. That distinction is important in how we look at enduring value rather than short-term value. It's how you develop an enduring supply chain and communities across the value chain."

Victoria: "This business has been my life, and when I think back, our family was trying to teach us the passion for the business that we have today. They were teaching us why it is special. As the business was getting bigger, they noticed how much harder it was for the family to be in touch with what was happening in the same way. In the beginning the family was visible on a regular basis at every site, but that's not possible in the same way at the scale that we are today. It is also what helped inform the Ombudsman programme that I launched and built into a global programme. An independent, confidential, informal and neutral resource, the Programme is available to all Associates. An alternative to formal communication channels such as

Line Managers and HR, it offers a safe place for Associates to seek guidance, voice concerns or discuss work-related matters. Our business has grown, and our people today are across the world, but through our Principles we are clear on the things that are important to us, and this is about a safe place where everyone can be listened to. And as a family business, we have sustained and kept it going, because we see that it benefits both engagement and retention over time. It's something that we believe in as a large family business."

You are a fourth-generation family business, with multiple generations represented in 150,000 Mars Associates around the world. There is a lot of intentional work that you do as a family, across generations, and that you invest in as a business. Can you share some of this with us?

Victoria: "Generations change. Expectations of generations are different from one to the next. And you have to accept that it's changing. In family businesses, as the family gets bigger and more complex, and the further away it is from the founder, the harder you have to work. You have to continue to work on keeping the family connected to the business in a different way and to who we are as an organisation – it's about what is going to make them proud."

Stephen: "The question is, is it the business or family that binds us, and the balance at any point in time might be different. Related to that a generational dialogue became important for myself, my sisters and my cousins, which led us to develop a vision for our generation. In the process we realised we needed to engage our own children – the next generation – and that caused us to start the

Family Assembly – in 2004. What originally started with an eye to organising ourselves as a generation, eventually morphed into an imperative to bring us together multigenerationally. Interestingly and perhaps, even more importantly, was what came out of that – which was how the next generation started to work together, at a much earlier stage than we did, and in ways that embraced their differences, their styles etc., in a much more open and candid way, and far sooner than we ever did, or perhaps even do now."

Victoria: "We always have generational work going on, from the G5 owners to annual family meetings, where we bring everyone together, and that my children have been part of over the years. There is a lot of work happening in team building, communications, conflict resolution. It takes time to bond and bind. We work hard on ourselves. That's important, because it makes us more effective when we look at what is happening in the business, and to the future of business. It's not how big and profitable we are, it's who we are. It's our reputation as an employer, as an organisation, and in how we treat the environment. It's what makes you proud to be connected to this business – and wanting to continue to put the work and energy into what it takes to keep a family business going."

> **"The world we want tomorrow starts with how we do business today".**
>
> Mars Purpose statement

The Mars Compass guides the long-term strategy of the business and measures progress against medium term and day-to-day decisions. It operates across four quadrants:

Financial performance – *top-tier performance that gives us the freedom to create the world we want tomorrow.*

Quality growth – *momentum and growth of our brands and categories, and the exploration of new opportunities to help us grow for the next 100 years.*

Positive societal impact – *our commitment to helping people, their pets and the planet thrive, which in part we will deliver through our Sustainable in a Generation Plan.*

Trusted partner – *trust we earn based on our actions; the response we see from stakeholders of how we are living up to our commitments and their expectations of Mars as a business.*

The Compass is one of the manifestations of the family coming together in service of the next generations of the business. Can you share with us why that came about at a defining point in time, and the role that it plays today?

Frank: "The Compass is still relatively new. This was our creation of what we wanted our legacy to be as a generation. Our purpose is 'The world we want tomorrow starts with how we do business today.' 'How' was the operative word when we defined it and is what separates Mars. It's about 'how' we do things. The Principles are the 'how'."

Victoria: "That long-term view matters – we're not making decisions for quick quarterly profits. At the beginning, my father and uncle had no need for shareholder objectives as they filled all the governance positions. The Compass is a tool to communicate our expectations and to measure our progress. It is holistic. That's what's so magical about our Compass and what has worked so well. It's about what is going to keep us engaged and connected. The return, which is financial and emotional, is worth the energy and effort that we put into maintaining it. This is where the continued family engagement and work matters to keep this going. We're working hard to do the right thing – to do good things. That's also why I work with The Livelihoods Fund for Family Farming as part of a wider ecosystem towards some of these solutions."

Stephen: "As a family business, we have always tended to be quite private. Perhaps one of the things that we still don't do as well as we could, is to tell the world who we are. Wanting to know who I am working for is true for a lot of our Associates, and for younger Associates, that's especially true. They are looking to each other for that peer endorsement of the business they are working for. Especially in their expectations of a multinational. We need to attract the best and brightest, and to do that we need to tell our story, and that story will have a number of components. One of them is surely a company's approach to sustainability. Because of the critical nature of this issue to our business, we have a programme that's best in class – we call it our Sustainable in a Generation Plan, and this is something that without doubt is important to existing and potential Associates."

Frank: "Mars is a storytelling culture. It's not a written-down culture. And it's the legacy of each group/generation to teach people through how they have lived the Principles. We are getting better about handovers and knowledge transfer. One of the things that we're doing is a video series with senior leaders to capture their stories. The idea is to use storytelling to share that knowledge and carry forward our legacy. That's part of what we're doing in looking at ways to tell our stories through the generations in the business. Today we have more Associates in hospitals than we do in factories, so it's how you make it more inclusive. You hear the word 'we' used a lot across generations at Mars. There is a reason why people who moved on from Mars still call themselves 'Martians'. If you talk with retirees, people who were with us for up to 30 years in the business, they will ask you "how are *we* doing?".

THE PENTLAND GROUP

The responsibility of ownership

London

The Pentland Group is the family business behind some of the most well-known and successful sports, outdoor and lifestyle brands, including Speedo, Berghaus, ellesse and Canterbury. Established in 1932 as a shoe business, the business has since grown to encompass a portfolio of brands alongside the family office and investment arm, Pentland Capital. In 1981, the family was an early investor in Reebok. At the time, Reebok was not the recognised and valued brand that we know today, and it was an investment which proved pivotal in propelling the growth of the business. Today, the company employs over 1400 people worldwide, with Pentland Group businesses employing over 76,000 people. Through its commitments to sustainability and fair trade, including establishing the Pentland Centre for Sustainability in Business at Lancaster University, Pentland has been recognised internationally in a number of leading awards for the Group's commitment to sustainability, human rights and the environment throughout the value chain.

We spoke with **Andy Rubin, third-generation family member, Chair of Pentland Brands and Deputy Chair of Pentland Group, Charlie Rubin, fourth-generation family member and Vice President, Pentland Capital, Katie Cohen, fourth-generation family member and Head of Marketing for ellesse, and Belinda Deery, Chief Human Resources Officer.**

As a family business, you talk about "Pioneering brands that make life better." Andy, could you share more with us about that sense of purpose and what it continues to mean today?

Andy: "Purpose is central for us in building on from the original founding focus and passion of our grandparents, Berko and Minnie. Communicating this to the next generation of the family is vitally important, ensuring that we don't lose or dilute that sense of 'why' over time. For the next generation family members, we need to be clear, as family owners, about why we are in business and what we stand for. It's about how that story is carried forward."

"Something that we have found helpful is to be very clear and transparent on roles and responsibilities. I think about the Three-Circle model of the family system – developed by Renato Tagiuri and John Davis in the 1970s. The Venn diagram is a powerfully simple way of articulating the spheres of business, family and ownership, and everyone's roles and remits within and across those spheres. We recently invested in the next generation of the family's education with a two-year programme, designed to upskill them all in the fundamentals of a family business, from the roles in the company, to the operations, to the responsibility of ownership. What was important was helping them understand what it means to be a responsible owner. We have an ethos of humility and a strong work ethic, and we wanted to instil that mindset of being humble and hardworking."

Charlie, Katie, as fourth-generation family members you are both now involved in the business. What are some of the ways in which you both actively facilitate intergenerational collaboration?

Charlie: "My direct boss is my grandfather, so where Katie is managing largely across adjacent generations (Gen Z and young Millennials), my grandfather and I have a two-generations gap. There are definite differences – one of those is pattern recognition, as I realise what my grandfather has seen over 65–70 years and how he applies that to today's context. I marry that with my experiences of the fundamental changes in the fundraising environment, in family offices, angels etc., as well as tech advancements. Another truth in all of this is his legendary deal-making experience. As a Millennial, thanks to my grandfather, I gain his experience of what good dealmaking looks like. It's a visual that I always have of him in the back of my mind."

> **"The culture helps."**
>
> Katie Rubin, Head of Marketing, ellesse

Katie: "The culture helps. As Head of Marketing for ellesse and as a Millennial, the team that I work with are young Millennials or Gen Zs. It's natural for our brand, which skews to a young consumer, and that's valuable because they are potentially consumers of the brand. There is a different value exchange in the workplace with our youngest gens – and that is already different to how I looked at it when I first started work. The question is how you manage the different views. That's why having a clear strategy with clear objectives and guiding principles is crucial – you know what you're holding people to account for.

Above all, there is an understanding behind everything that we do – a super supportive culture which everyone feels and experiences. Even before I went into this role, and since the generations have shifted in the workplace, the company was always good at that. We genuinely care. We also have flat hierarchies, as part of that reflection of our culture."

Charlie: "Culture lives at a top level in the business. Having the right culture allows generations to work well together. I have worked in and experienced hierarchical structures, and, having an open non-hierarchical culture, as we do, works better from an intergenerational perspective."

The Pentland Youth Collective is a commitment that you have made more recently, as a collaborative connecting perspectives both within and outside the business from a generational lens. Could you share more about how this came about, and how it is working?

Belinda: "The Youth Collective manifested from a number of things. The business has successfully had the benefit of a lot of self-generated and self-managed special-interest groups. We have a thriving men's mental health community led by a number of our Gen X men, and most of our communities tend to be multigenerational and diverse. These have resulted in great connectivity around the business, and we wanted to continue to let it be quite organic. We felt that a generational lens could augment what we had, and we formalised the Pentland Collective, as an umbrella to the special-interest groups. The purpose is to seek and gain their qualitative and quantitative input to help inform decision making, and it's building from there."

"Alongside the 50 young changemakers who are part of our wider communities network, the Collective is composed of 35 Pentland Brands employees from internal D&I networks. They represent a broad number of the markets that we are in, including China, India, Australia, New Zealand, Hong Kong, Vietnam, the UK, Germany and the US. They are broadly Gen Z and Millennial, and each of those 35 have groups behind them that extend into the workforce. We are also curious to get their lens on looking ahead at the 'weak signals' – at what we might need to consider in the longer-term future or have more depth on. There is no governance mandate. We haven't constructed it as a board – it's an advisory body, but giving some structure to it was important, as there is more vested interest in the value exchange and contribution."

And what are you starting to realise from the youth collective?

Belinda: "One of the areas that I was curious to explore was rising generations and their expectations on work – in particular, understanding their perspectives on the workplace, on hybrid working and wellbeing. We were also looking at our reward strategy and even physical currency – for example, what's the next generation perspective on rewards and quid pro quo? For some of the younger Gen Zs, their first move into the workplace has been on the back of virtual education through the pandemic. One of the big moves we're making is moving our HQ and main office to be in a location that will be more accessible to both current and future employees, and we really want to understand how we can make best use of that space."

"As a business, we want a much stronger voice around sustainability and positive business goals. It's increasingly hard to find a place of consumer truth around our desire and need to manage our operations on the planet more sustainably – aligning what consumers really believe and where they are prepared to put their money to do something about it. It's about finding a route through so that we make our contribution in the right way, and this is a place where the Collective can play a part. The output of the Youth Collective is really powerful – and there is a lot of similarity – the congruence of views is much stronger than rhetoric would lead you to believe. No matter what generation, it's the human aspect of the lens or issue – they care in the same way."

> **"Brand relevance is about how we connect across generations."**
>
> Charlie Rubin Vice President, Pentland Capital

Given the spaces that you're in, as a business, across sports and lifestyle, the brands that you have in your portfolio also go hand in hand with how they connect to different generations. Could you share some examples of that, as you're connecting the culture of the business to consumer culture?

Charlie: "Brand relevance is about how we connect across generations. ellesse in the 90s had a very different profile, and now it's a brand that Gen Zs wear. One example is a project that we worked on for the football brand Mitre, exploring how we would target Gen Z. The hypothesis was that Gen Z didn't know who Mitre was, because the brand simply wasn't on their radar and therefore wasn't part of the conversation. The action we took as a result was to amplify our investment with Millennials in strengthening their connection to the brand, knowing that would cascade to Gen Z."

Katie: "We're doing something similar at ellesse. The conclusion is that we need to target a bit older and then to engage the next generation from there. We're also partnering with fashion graduates and young designers, which has been useful in introducing another creative perspective."

Andy: "We are obsessed about customer centricity, and that in turn drives our ability to ensure our brands remain relevant. Berghaus is a good example of a brand well loved by a loyal audience. Retaining that loyalty is vitally important, as we connect the brand to the next generations through collaborations and adjacencies with other worlds, such as fashion and music."

Belinda: "We are currently using the Youth Collective with some of the brands to explore product innovation, and some of the brands are starting to tap into from a multigenerational perspective. Berghaus is a good example. Berghaus has had two phases – Gen X was at the formation of the brand, and it's having its second wave with their children."

Are there any generational patterns in the brands that people are working for in the portfolio?

Belinda: "Our people span four generations across 18 countries, and that multigenerational make-up varies across the Group. For example, we have a longstanding distribution workforce in the UK where the majority of employees are Gen X and Boomers. By contrast, we're building a data and tech hub in India where everyone is under 34. The portfolio lends itself to opportunity in different spaces for different generations."

Belinda: "Speedo is a truly global brand which is universal in its appeal. It's often a brand that you learn to swim with and that you grow up with. To some extent, it's seen as one of those more democratic brands. People often remember it as the brand on the clocks of most swimming pools. The brand operates across both recreational and performance, and its pinnacle, of course, is in elite swim, which starts at an early age. Equally, there is a large community of swim coaches in their 60s and 70s. We have quite a few elite swimmers working for the brand, which ensures all products are both authentic and highly functional."

"Our Kickers brand, which is licensed for the UK, is targeted at children, although they're not the direct purchasers. It's another example of the adjacent generations that Charlie and Katie talked about. And the team that we typically have on the brand is aligned to the brand personality, which is young, dynamic and fun. It tends to attract younger generations and people earlier in their careers. This is a strength of the portfolio, as it allows us to be more intentional in how we think about both career pathways, generational lenses and life stages across our business."

Katie: "The ways in which you can be involved is a key strength at Pentland. Having grown up with a more singular view on the brands, now that I am working in the business, I have a better appreciation of what we do, and of what everyone has the opportunity to do."

The metaphors of 'bridging' and acting as a 'sounding board' have come up a lot in our conversation. Communications obviously, are central to that – what does that look like in practice?

Andy: "I am involved in a number of Family Business networks, where we share best practice and challenges. A consistent theme in those discussions is communications. Themes such as 'false harmony' are discussed as this can be a danger to family business, and it's vital that we are all able to bring different perspectives to the table very openly and constructively. 'Psychological safety' is another theme that I find interesting in thinking about how we create the conditions for everyone to speak up, to be heard and to thrive."

"Gen Xers are often taking on these bridging roles between generations, facilitating the dialogue and understanding. Conduits are very important in how we think about creating better intergenerational understanding. We have a non-exec who also plays an important role in this context."

Katie: "It's important to keep opening up the conversation across generations in the family and in the business. We have always been close as brother and sister, so that flow of conversation early on was already there."

Charlie: "That really comes to mean something when you think about how many lives you touch, with employees and with consumers. That openness in communication is what enables us to make the decisions we need to make today, that will go on to impact so many people over time. When you're in a position to make longer-term decisions, you feel that sense of responsibility. There is a sense of legacy – and the responsibility to generations before us, and for the next generations."

"Words are events, they do things, change things. They feed understanding or emotion back and forth and amplify it."

Ursula K. Le Guin

An iconic writer known for her science fiction, Le Guin was also a far-reaching essayist. In this chapter, we spotlight organisations across global business and civil society who are establishing next gen platforms to feed and amplify that understanding across generations.

6

Next Generation Boards

We need to ask better questions, as Dr. Tomas Chamorro-Premuzic reminds us in *I, Human*. However, asking better questions is only part of the solution. What we need in leadership discussions and in the boardroom is a diversity of perspectives and experiences to engage with those questions and come with pragmatic answers. While the needle is shifting, diversifying the shape of boards and leadership teams remains an ongoing challenge. And it will require a diversity of solutions. And so, we turn our focus in this chapter to a valuable platform that has quietly been gaining in traction and recognition – the next generation board.

'Next generation boards' are by no means brand new. These are Boards and Councils introduced and adopted by organisations looking to inject the insight and influence of a younger or cross-generational lens. Where the non-profit sector had started to embrace Youth Advisory Boards and Youth Councils, in the corporate world they were far from the norm. It was thanks to the transformative era of one of the most valuable luxury brands in the world, that the concept received a PR boost. That brand was Gucci, with the launch of their next generation board – The Shadow Comex – and we will go on to unpack the context and the case study.

The public endorsement of Gucci's next generation board by its then CEO Marco Bizzarri, was important as we start to put into context the rise of these boards in the corporate world. Even where companies were putting them into operation, they were not necessarily being talked about. Where they were evident in the civil society sector, they also tended to be more prevalent in organisations dedicated to, or impacting young people, most notably in areas such as: education and career mobility (such as The EY Foundation); the creative industries (such as The Royal Shakespeare Company); and human rights organisations (such as Amnesty International, PLAN, Save the Children and UNICEF UK).

As we look at adoption in the corporate and wider world, the following is by no means intended as a definitive time-line, but it puts this into context and gives a sense of what was starting to emerge in the adoption of next generation boards across markets and industries: Aramco's Young Leaders Advisory Board (2011), Gucci's Shadow Comex (2015), Accor's Shadow Committee (2016), The Financial Times Next Generation Board (2020), Interbrand's Horizon Board (2020), The EU Commission's Youth Sounding Board (2021), The OECD's (Organisation for Economic Co-operation and Development) Youthwise Board (2021) and Liberty Global's Youth Council (2023).

These boards manifest in different shapes and forms, but their respective naming and framing sends a key signal around the highest common denominator – of their pur-pose in affording a different perspective through a genera-tional lens. And their business logic is further supported by the evidence of the generational gap. As NYU Stern's Alison Taylor states: *". . . these are powerful signals about shifts in society, many Gen Z concerns about culture, incentives and leadership in the private sector are valid, and it is bewildering to me how few mainstream firms are adjusting their approaches and business models to appeal* to a new generation."[1] We are not suggesting that the introduction of a next generation board is the entire solution, but it is increasingly evident that it has a strategic role to play in closing that gap and in its wider halo effects both across and beyond an organisation. As we deep dive into a series of case studies and conversations, we demonstrate the value of next generation boards through the lenses of five generations.

Multipliers of shared value

Where the value of next generation boards is already being recognised, it is by companies and organisations who understand that the value is both shared and multiple. Investing in these platforms is investing in levels of cultural, collaborative and competitive advantage. In cases such as Accor and Gucci, we chart next generation boards whose purpose manifests explicitly in connecting a generation of employees with a generation of customers. We also know that they play a valuable role across the company – while membership of these next generation boards and committees is often the purview of a few, they succeed, in many respects, as wider accumulators of value. They are *sustained* commitments – breaking the cycle of the 'project and initiative fatigue' that we referenced earlier, and as documented by Gartner and others. They are *legacy* commitments, as they rotate through a series of cohorts, with each board passing on the torch of knowledge, experience and impact to the next. And, because these are leadership-level commitments, there is a wider halo effect with employees across the organisation, and with future employees, as we see next generation boards show up as part of the employer brand proposition and as a significant contributor both to talent retention and attraction.

Effectively, these boards are a new operating platform of shared value, which have far-reaching benefits for the company, for the board as a collective, and for board members as individuals:

- *A practical contribution to this new era of collective leadership and to longer-term decision-making*
- *An agile investment in future leaders, and the pipeline of board talent*
- *Accelerators and amplifiers of engagement in the organisation*
- *Modelling and role-modelling progress on diversity and inclusion*
- *Increased legitimacy with both employees and consumers*

> **" We are writing different chapters to try to change an organization and culture on a daily basis . . . You need to see things in different ways, because the industry and the world are changing too fast."**[2]
>
> Marco Bizzarri (President and CEO of Gucci from 2015 to 2023)

As we will see here, and across the deeper case studies and conversations that we explore, their purpose and benefits range and vary from platforms for innovation to catalysts for cultural and digital transformation. A red thread that runs throughout is the vital and valuable role of the next generation board in representing the voice of its generation(s) to help inform strategic business imperatives and planning.

Gucci's meteoric rise from 2015 to 2019 also recorded it as one of the fastest-growing brands amongst the 100 most valuable brands in the world.[3] Part of the brand's ability to connect into the cultural and Millennial zeitgeist was attributed to how it was connecting to its own culture and better understanding the next generation of consumers through the generational lens of its employees.

That context is important, because it was in 2015 that Gucci established its Shadow Comex – a shadow board composed of Millennials, with whom CEO Marco Bizzarri and the senior team met on a regular basis. As Bizzarri shared in an interview when the Shadow Comex was two years into its tenure: *The task is either discussing the same topics that we discuss in the normal meeting with executives, or giving me ideas on different processes.*"[4] That intergenerational listening went on to play a key role at a time when the brand was seeking to engage with a younger generation of consumers and making that same connection with its employees. As Fast Company evidenced in 2018: *"62% of Gucci's more than $8 billion in sales came from the under-35 set, a demographic that is generally harder for luxury brands to capture, given the high price points of their products."*[5] The Shadow Comex was amongst a series of commitments within Gucci's transformative Culture of Purpose. However, as Bizzarri was consistently vocal in speaking to the market about its value, it became one of the most recognised manifestations of its Culture of Purpose. This was a brand, in many respects, being transformed by Millennials, for Millennials.

Providing "a wider range of views"[6] was the driving force behind the Shadow Board set up by RenewableUK, the leading not for profit renewable energy trade association for wind, wave and tidal power industries in the United Kingdom. The membership comprises a collective of businesses, employing over 250,000 people, from large international energy companies to smaller companies and emerging brands. The Shadow Board "not only reflects its commitment to improving gender and ethnic diversity but also reflects geographical and technological diversity that represents a broader range of its membership." They go on to emphasise the importance of diversity of skillset across their Shadow Board members: "They offer high levels of expertise in areas such as in electrical engineering, project management, law, marketing, asset management, business development, environmental management and public affairs."[7] The shared value of the Shadow Board is in the diversity of sparring and thinking helping to inform the ongoing success and evolution of the renewable sector.

For LG, one of the leading family-run conglomerates in South Korea, it is about investing in a series of cross-generational commitments across the organisation, from their Junior Board, designed to represent the voice of employees, to LG IdeaPot, a platform that sits across the entire organisation as an ongoing source of collective intelligence. The Shadow Committee representing the 'MZ generation' – a mix of Millennials and Gen Z employees – is purposed towards informing product ideation, design and innovation.

The European Commission's Directorate-General for International Partnerships (DG-INTPA) holds a far-reaching remit across some of the most pressing agendas of our times: climate, environment and energy; digital infrastructure; gender equality; human development; migration;

peace and governance; sustainable growth and jobs. Under the leadership of the Commissioner for International Partnerships Jutta Urpilainen, the DG-INTPA works together with partner countries across the world "to achieve sustainable development and reduce poverty, promote democracy, human rights, and the rule of law across the world."

As part of that agenda, the DG-INTPA established the Youth Sounding Board (YSB), which was set up in 2021 "to create a real, fundamental, long-lasting change in how the EU engages with young people in its development cooperation."[8] Their contribution is to "make EU action more participatory, relevant and effective for young people in EU partner countries, across all political priorities."[9] Part of their remit includes informing and shaping both the agenda and partnerships.

Importantly, members act as catalysts of much wider conversations, in canvassing opinion within and across their own networks, as well as in their collaborations with other youth organisations across the EU, and across their country network. The selection process lends further context to the mutual value of the Board and structuring of the members as a collective. Two of the key criteria on which candidates are selected are "Experience in youth participation and youth empowerment" and "Outreach and youth engagement skills and experience". The prominence and value of this platform is such that the 2023–2025 cohort received over 4500 applications from more than 150 countries.

Co-creative solutions, sustainable thinking and systemic action are integral to the shape of the YSB's work, which is carried forward from cohort to cohort. The 2023–2025 cohort is involved in the implementation and dissemination of the EU Youth Action Plan, which was co-created by the founding YSB. This sustainable thinking defines the trajectory of projects that the members are working on in parallel: diversity and inclusion, intergenerational dialogue, leadership and community-building and outreach to young people. As the DG-INTPA stated: "The outcomes of the projects informed the design of DG-INTPA actions and programming on youth." "The continuation of the YSB is one of the institutional commitments foreseen in the Youth Action Plan (YAP) in EU external action to step up meaningful youth participation. Adopted in October 2022, the YAP is putting forward a vision and partnership with young people as essential actors of change for more democratic, equal, inclusive and peaceful societies."[10]

Sustained change through sustained investment

With more organisations looking to integrate more effective intergenerational dialogue in decision-making processes, a key investment is in the skills needed to support these collectives of people who are often coming together for the first time in this way. This is mission critical in the non-profit sector, where youth advisory boards tend to skew younger, and where they are often working together in a different context to that of next generation boards in corporate organisations. In the majority of corporate next generation boards, there is a unifying element in the brand, as employees may be drawn from disparate parts of a company, but they are all working for the same brand in their day-to-day. With non-profits, the reverse is often true, where young people are uniting under the aegis of a given organisation but are otherwise separate in their day-to-day.

And this is where investment is key to setting the foundations and sustained success to drive the competitive, cultural and collaborative advantage of next generation boards. That investment is something that we are seeing increasingly in organisations and companies, as we go on to demonstrate in the case studies and conversations. The EY Foundation in the UK is taking this to a next level, in the ambition driving its Communications Academy. Designed to address the *range* of support that young people need, as identified by the young people that they are supporting, the ambition of the Communications Academy is to equip young people from a low-income background with the skills, experience, and confidence to promote their voice and to influence decision-makers. By ensuring that the views of those who are often overlooked are heard, Ewan Bennie, Director of Communications and Influence, sees this as an opportunity to transform the way organisations work with young people: *"By identifying the specific communication barriers facing young people from a low socio-economic background – and how they can be overcome – we hope to demonstrate the potential impact of this new skills training model to amplify their voice in employment-related decision-making across the country."*

Investment in corporate next generation boards takes different forms, but one of the common threads is two-way mentoring between the board members and leadership, as embedded in both the FT's Next Generation Board and

Interbrand's Horizon Board. Above all, it is the mindset that makes the difference – in seeing these platforms as both a sustained and systemic commitment to intergenerational collaboration, and as a wider investment in the development of rising talent. As executive search firm Spencer Stuart evidences: ". . . appointing more youthful board members remains an underutilized opportunity."[11] There is a very intentional profile that RenewableUK speaks to in the selection of their Shadow Board members: "They are at a senior level in their companies but they do not have Board-level experience."[10] In the same way that the EY Foundation is looking to the sector-wide benefit of its Communications Academy, we should look to the wider benefit of next generation boards in addressing the challenge of developing and diversifying the talent pipeline for boards.

Next generation boards are proof positive of practical and progressive benefits and outcomes of intergenerational thinking. Agile, action-oriented, defining new norms in diversity and becoming models of collaboration, think of next gen boards as accelerators of future leaders, as role models of diverse collectives and as influencers of governance and the shape of boards to come.

If this has inspired you to think about exploring a next generation board or youth advisory in your organisation, we close out with a summary of common principles and practical advice, followed by a series of case studies and conversations that we hope will capture your hearts and minds as much as they did ours.

Setting up your next generation board

A major motivation for writing this book was to open-source inspiring stories from our journey and work, sparking ideas that might be helpful for your organisation. Benchmarking the next generation boards and youth advisories from our body of research and our own lived experience across the world, we have distilled a guideline designed to help translate some of those ideas into practice for your organisation:

> **Motivations and purpose.** When considering the 'why' behind setting up a next gen board, what is so useful and liberating is that there is no single definition – the overriding factor is to define what is most relevant and helpful to your organisation. Common drivers from our research and experience tend to begin with one or more of the following objectives: Organisational or cultural transformation; Business model reinvention or radical changes to process; Better engagement of stakeholder groups (e.g., younger people in the organisation); Boosting diversity of thinking through enabling a more diverse group than the Board or ExCo itself to have influence. Above all, be clear in outlining the objectives and expectations.

> **Terms and tenures:** 12–18 months is a minimum-average for each cohort to form and norm and to make an impact.

> **Size of the board:** Following the principles and practice of good board effectiveness, the most effective tend to average 10–12 members.

Shaping the board: Be clear in how you are constructing a multidimensional and diverse board, and identify the skills, knowledge, and expertise that you are looking for.

Selection processes: How you inform the process is one of the most important decisions and determinants. An inclusive approach to both application criteria and selection processes is key – think open applications accessible to all, versus selective nomination by the few. Good selection processes also incorporate debiasing in the process and a focus on diversity of character in forming a high-performing collective.

Structures and roles: How to facilitate fair and mutually effective contributions is a question reflected on by everyone who sets up a next gen board. As ever, context is key, especially where the board may be operating remotely from locations across a country or region or across the world. Simple moves in establishing clear principles and processes to facilitate engagement go a long way to promote individual and shared contribution and can take a number of forms, from Committee roles to connecting members with different business units in the organisation.

A learning mindset: The importance of investing for success is a common thread through the global body of next generation and youth advisory boards that we have explored. As you may be setting out to do this for the first time, a learning mindset is crucial in the foundation work and in the founding year and remains an integral mechanism throughout. Smart use of mentoring, feedback loops and communication across the organisation will underpin platforms that are successful and sustainable.

The benefits are multiple, as the case studies and conversations go on to demonstrate and celebrate. Next generation boards and advisories are already leading the way as some of the most diverse collectives within organisations. They are creating spaces for bolder and more constructive dialogue, which is all the more vital, where spaces for constructive dissent, in many contexts across business and society, have become fewer and further between. They also exercise the voice of the many to the power of the few. In the corporate dynamic, especially, there is a wider role in the engagement and halo effect across the business – as evidenced widely with the Financial Times Next Generation Board, through its collaboration with existing Employee Resource Groups (ERGs) across the group. They are an investment at multiple levels. At an individual member level, they are platforms for accelerating rising leadership. At a collective level, there is the value of the peer group and the 'network effect' for life. At a business and board level, the benefits are in living evidence, in their ability to catalyse, accelerate and amplify sustainable and systemic change.

THE EY FOUNDATION

Head and Heart

London

THE EY Foundation (EYF) is an independent charity founded by EY, the global professional services firm. It has a focus on young people from low-income backgrounds supporting them with access to paid work experience, employability skills and career guidance. It believes that impact is best created by working on both sides of the labour market at the same time.

Having an independent majority and age diverse board and Youth Advisory Board (YAB) from the start has helped EYF to pioneer fresh approaches to supporting employers in diversifying talent pipelines, in developing its programmes and in creating innovative high impact volunteer-based approaches to delivery. The EYF operates across five generations – through the young people that it serves, the team, the volunteers, its trustees and patrons.

High impact charities focussed on supporting young people need to have the young people that they support at the heart of all they do, but the founders of EYF wanted to be bolder than that. *"When we were founding EYF we wanted young people at the head as well as the heart. We wanted them to get involved in shaping the charity, in making the big decisions and challenging conventional thinking. We had no preconceived ideas about how this might work and were prepared to take the risk to learn about how best to achieve our goal."* EYF Founding Chair Patrick Dunne

The charity and, more importantly, the young people that it supports have benefited greatly from this decision. From an initial approach of putting three young people on the board and establishing a Youth Council, EYF has constantly learnt and adapted. Chris Achiampong is one of those first three young people on the Board and was Chair of EYF's first Youth Council (the predecessor to the YAB). Now at IBM, he recalls his experience of EYF at this formative stage:

"When I came into EYF I didn't know what I was going to do next. It was a life changing experience for me. After trying for professional football, I was at a crossroads in my life. EYF was a great platform to grow and develop my skills and experience. The experience of being on one of the programmes and the boost from being involved in helping to shape the charity as a trustee and Chair of the first Youth Council propelled me forward. Now I've been at IBM for seven years in a role I love, working on Signature Accounts in IBM's Cloud sales business."

"Getting involved in big early decisions, chairing meetings, aligning the wide range of views, pitching to employer partners, raising money and speaking on a range of plat-forms was brilliant experience at such a young age. It was so motivating. It gave me skills and confidence and a window on the world I never would have had otherwise."

Why does this matter?

Since inception the three big questions the YAB have focussed on, working with the EYF board and leadership team, have been:

1. What do young people need right now to help them succeed in their careers?
2. How can we reach more young people digitally and in other ways?
3. How can we improve our programmes?

> **"These commitments – bringing people into decision making, acting on it and taking it seriously – take a lot of trust."**
>
> Laura McLay, former YAB member

Youth Advisory Board members have the opportunity to provide input and challenge to all significant plans before they go to the EYF board. They also represent the Foundation in a variety of ways from events to meetings with key influencers, including government in the youth and employability space.

Former YAB Co-Chair Maria Owusu-Mensah, now a Trading and Shipping Commercial Graduate at BP, values the authenticity of the YAB and how it develops YAB members' confidence to express their views to influence decisions: *"What's important is being intentional about creating room – for youth voice. That's been the best thing – an opportunity to make genuine impact within the lives of young people. It's also been a great personal development story. I wasn't confident – and now I am. The space is more open and collaborative than hierarchical, which has been so important to us."* Her Co-Chair at the time Ebenezer Odubanjo, now a degree apprentice at JP Morgan reinforced this point: *"It's a genuine platform for anyone – an enabler."* Laura McLay an EYF YAB member from 2019 to 2021 emphasised the importance of trust in the success of the YAB: *"These commitments – bringing people into decision-making, acting on it and taking it seriously – take a lot of trust."*

There are numerous examples evidencing that EYF is getting the impact it seeks from its YAB through better decisions, innovation and authenticity throughout its latest published Impact Report. The work that EYF's YAB did during the pandemic was essential to ensuring that EYF not only maintained but increased its momentum and impact. Two strong examples are the work that the YAB has done to inform EYF's digital strategy and support programmes, and the collaboration between EYF and Ofcom, the UK's Communications Regulator, in researching, raising awareness and informing a more inclusive use of technology to develop skills and improve employability prospects.

From inputting into EYF's race commitments, to having a lens on the right balance of physical and virtual delivery, as well as contributing to the design of EYF's sector-based programmes and research projects, the YAB has added significantly to the effectiveness of what the Foundation does and delivers. Charity sector icon and EYF Patron Dame Mary Marsh makes two important points about what EYF's approach is doing for the sector, and what the YAB commitment did at a wider level across the EY UK business.

"What EYF has done in 10 years is remarkable – it's built a way of doing things that works and has created a mass of opportunities. The YAB was a differentiator from the start of the Foundation – I don't know other foundations who have done it so well. YAB members have gained experience that they would have otherwise been challenged to gain, and it's a great two-way process – I learn so much when I meet with the YAB."

"I believe it is also enriching EY's thinking more broadly and has helped to transform the business. Just look at the progress they have made in their approach to apprenticeships as well as graduates. It has reframed their perspectives as well as those of other employers."

Hywel Ball, EY UK Chair and UK & Ireland Managing Partner, evidenced this from EY's perspective: *"For anyone working in business, one of the most important questions you can ask yourself is: 'What's next?' Having the ability to absorb information from multiple sources to inform your perspective, identify the potential opportunities and challenges of the future and to create a long-term strategy sets apart the most successful leaders. The Youth Advisory Board at the EY Foundation is one of the sources we use to directly hear feedback, perspectives, and guidance from those we are trying to create opportunity for. As EY continues to explore new pathways for talent, widen our recruitment net and support initiatives which foster education and opportunity, the EY Foundation YAB will remain an effective mechanism to support our purpose of building a better working world."*

By having a YAB member on each of the Board's sub-committees, YAB members have not only contributed greatly to making better decisions but have also learnt useful board skills increasing their own potential in the process. During her YAB tenure Laura McLay was also a member of EYF's Nominations Committee. She emphasised the nature of the contribution and the value that can be had from such a role as it evolves and changes as you go through it: *"What being an EYF YAB member meant to me has changed over a couple of years. Before I started it was about taking an opportunity to make change in an area that I cared about – careers education in schools. I didn't have the tools myself to do this, while EYF had the resources, staff and knowledge. As a YAB member, I realised the YAB's power lay more specifically in helping EYF to become even more relevant to young people. Two years on from my tenure, and looking at the YAB from an external perspective, my view of the YAB's role has changed again, to see it as a symbol to others of the importance of age diversity in decision-making."*

A decade of evolution

The core principle of "Head and Heart" has remained the same even though EYF's YAB operating model has adapted considerably over the last decade. It has been a constant learning process, but the culture of try, feedback, learn and adapt has enabled EYF's YAB to evolve successfully. Today the EYF YAB is a group of 12 young people, aged 16–25 from across England and Scotland who act as advisors to EYF. Each YAB cohort has a two-year term and supports the next cohort in the transition.

"I have a big thing about the word 'legacy' as it means its impact will continue into the future . . ."

Each cohort's legacy project reinforces the impact focus as well as giving the cohort a significant contribution that they can be identified with. For the first cohort this was to get a Youth Council up and running with an effective model; for the second it was to provide significant input to EYF's digital strategy. The third was focused on supporting EYF to provide the maximum impact for young people through the pandemic. Ebenezer Odubanjo Co-Chair of the latest cohort describes the 2023 YAB legacy project: *"This was a YAB organised and facilitated event in Manchester supported by the EYF team, bringing employers and young people together to take a solutions-focussed approach to the future of work. I have a big thing about the word 'legacy' as it means its impact will continue into the future, and we hope future cohorts will build upon what we do."*

Key to the success of the YAB has been the investment in supporting them as well as providing development opportunities. As the charity has grown, the support model has evolved and includes far more today than 10 years ago. One example of this is investment in learning and development, and in face-to-face meetings (as members are based across the UK). As Jodie McNally, EYF's Chief Programmes Officer, who has been responsible for the continuous adaptation of the YAB believes: *"If you embark on establishing a YAB, it's important to make sure you have the right resources in place. We found that having a member of the team with dedicated time for supporting the YAB has been essential in getting us to where we are today and demonstrates our commitment as an organisation. I often get asked 'What are the key ingredients to a successful YAB?', and I think the infrastructure part is the main thing – you need to be prepared for everything else to be fluid! We're now on our fourth iteration of the YAB, and the structure, ways of working and focus have all been slightly different each time as we continue to learn, listen and adapt."*

The YAB itself has also proven to be an effective mechanism for dealing with the challenges that young members face taking on important commitments at such a critical and logistically challenging time in their lives. As Chris Achiampong put it: *"The biggest challenge always felt like time. It takes time to collaborate. Not just the time for formal meetings; it's all the other time taken up in preparing for them, canvassing views and so on. Putting together a problem statement and a great idea which might work takes time. Momentum can fizzle out. Everyone's heart is in the right place but prioritising can be difficult."*

Maria Owusu-Mensah agreed: *"When we get together in person the engagement is amazing. In those two years, people are going through significant changes – for example, going to university, starting their first job – lives are changing, and this has an impact. As a YAB leader, what works is trying to be intentional about the use of YAB members' time – it's easier to relate to them and to engage them if you do."*

We sum up in the words of EYF's CEO Lynne Peabody, who describes what the YAB means to her: *"Authenticity. That's what it means to me. For many years many charities have been paternalistic in how they operate, and without seeking feedback and input. That's where the YAB are important in sharing their input and views. They are bold – they give you a healthy dose of unvarnished honesty which you don't necessarily get from elsewhere. It's unfiltered and so valuable. On a personal level, I love seeing their individual growth. It works both ways – there's loads of stuff I have learned from them. It's a real two-way exchange. Perhaps people underestimate how valuable that is."*

FAST FACTS
THE EY FOUNDATION
YOUTH ADVISORY BOARD

Platform:	Youth Advisory Board
Geography:	UK
Industries:	Business, social and public sectors
Launched:	2014
Purpose:	To inform better decisions, innovation and to reinforce authenticity
Composition:	Open to young people aged 16–25 years
Members:	12
Tenure:	24 months
Alumni:	Four cohorts

MISSION 44

Together, we're unstoppable

London

"Together, we're unstoppable." It is a powerful and collective call to action that sets a sense of the expectation of the ambition of Mission 44 – a charitable foundation set up by Sir Lewis Hamilton, supporting bold organisations, leaders and ideas to reimagine the future and transform the lives of young people from underserved communities. Named after the number of Lewis's racing car, Mission 44's vision is to build a fairer, more inclusive future for young people around the world. Its core mission is to invest in solutions that empower young people to overcome social injustice and succeed. To achieve that, their work already spans a range of change-making, opening doors to careers within STEM and motorsport, and empowering young people to become an influential force for change. We spoke with **CEO, Jason Arthur to learn more about this young, but fast-moving organisation.**

What we see across so many of these conversations is something very powerful happening across and together *with* generations. How does this intergenerational discourse manifest across Mission 44? And how did the YAB begin?

The five-generation workplace is very much present in what we do and in how we work – through the YAB, the board, our mentors, patrons, partners and donors. It's a wide and diverse ecosystem. At the heart of our approach is a belief in genuine, meaningful diversity and inclusion. We believe young people should be at the heart of what we do – shaping decisions and helping us to achieve our strategy.

We're also conscious of the fact that youth empowerment can be a lazy narrative where the misperception is that having young people on board translates as them 'doing everything'. Not only does that fail to recognise the abilities and wisdom of other generations – it's not what young people want. They want to be able to contribute, but they shouldn't be expected to do it all. This is critical for us – getting the balance right of decision-making power and of driving change. And it's about who's making those decisions. It's a constant conversation.

Having the YAB was the plan from the outset. And making sure we had the capacity to work with young people in a meaningful way. They are a core part of how we see youth participation, consultation and constant dialogue. Importantly, our fund, where we're looking to give grants or to define research, will be shaped fully by young people.

> **"The Youth Advisory Board at Mission 44 is extraordinary. Each member brings a unique perspective that enriches our shared journey. I've witnessed first hand the incredible power that this group holds, united by a shared goal of reshaping the future."**
>
> Joshua Bruce, YAB Member

The language that we use is a powerful signal of an organisation's intent. Something that runs through our conversation, and throughout your communications as a foundation, is how you talk about "working with": *To transform the lives of young people from underrepresented* *and underserved communities, we have never believed that it is enough for us to work **for** them, treating them as passive recipients of our support. Rather, we need to work **with** young people, championing and empowering them to drive positive change. That's why, of all the things we have done over the last two years, setting up our Youth Advisory Board is undoubtedly one of the most important.* **Language is so powerful in setting the tone/expectations and creating a shared language.**

Yes, and our YAB play a key role here, informing campaigns and communications, and it will go further into policy engagement. We would like them to be at the forefront of that too. And there are two big areas that we're about to engage them on – our research strategy, and our expansion internationally, in Brazil and the US. We've already given our first two grants in the US. At a wider level, we are investing in young people as changemakers in new markets, and in how we inform our work in every country that we operate in.

This is also why we see this as an investment – we budgeted to pay for their time and for their development. The YAB spent their first month on how they would like to work with us and areas that they want support in, to inform the development plan. We have to think about the double benefit and the mutual learning – for us as an organisation and the difference that we're making, and for our YAB members as individuals. As you said, it's a multiplier effect.

"We're made even stronger with our brilliant Youth Advisory Board, who are guiding us at every step in our mission."

Sir Lewis Hamilton

Partners are an important part of your ecosystem. From within the F1 community and beyond, including brands such as NASA and Pirelli.

YAB members are actively engaging with our partners and play a role whenever we convene our partners. Some of the key questions that we have been addressing with Teach First are: how can we diversify the education system? How do we reduce the numbers of school exclusions? How do we reimagine what education might look like – through the lens of AI, or through assessment? And we're supporting more pathways into STEM and motorsport. With Sky we have a campaign around policy making. Our ambition is to grow and partner with other foundations in addressing systemic issues. We want to change systems. We want to be a convenor for change for good, which requires us to be bold and brave about some key topics.

An area that we want to develop further is how we influence organisations that aren't actively working with young people. The next step is to look at a meaningful youth participatory strategy in the partners and corporates. It's opening up a conversation around how our partners can translate some of the same principles in their organisations, and to diversify their leadership team. As you said, we see such diversity in the rise of Youth Advisory Boards and next generation boards. It's about how the authenticity of what matters to us also manifests in tangible ways with our partners.

When we reflect on the power of words, there is a simple, but powerful call to action that came out of the disability rights movement: "nothing about us without us". If we want to drive the change that we want to make for young people from underserved communities, I think there's a level of truth and power in that.

FAST FACTS

MISSION 44
YOUTH ADVISORY BOARD

Platform:	Youth Advisory Board
Geography:	UK
Industries:	STEM and motorsport
Launched:	2021
Purpose:	To shape strategy, influence decisions and build relationships
Composition:	Open to young people aged 16–24 years
Members:	13
Tenure:	Three years

THE FINANCIAL TIMES

Collaborate for success

London

One of the world's leading news organisations, the Financial Times was first established in 1888. Five years later, in a bid to differentiate itself from the black and white newsprint of its competitors, the FT began publishing the paper in the now inimitable light salmon Pantone. Today, the FT Group employs over 2700 people worldwide, including 700 journalists in 40 countries. The FT's Next Generation Board (NGB) programme was launched in 2020, composed of 10 emerging leaders representing different business areas and interests across the FT. We spoke with **Hannah Sarney, NGB Founder, Editorial Product Director and Executive Editor.**

Setting up a next gen board in a corporate context is still in its nascent stages. What was the founding vision for, and motivation behind doing this at the FT?

Initially the motivation was to try to create better connections for people and the kind of strategic connections that I had naturally in my role and benefited from. I was in an editorial role, but my job was to have conversations with people in every part of the business. The big benefit of being in that type of position is that it gives you a good understanding of the different strategies around the company. That broad insight was a huge advantage as I was able to connect the dots and bring people together and move things forward faster, and I started thinking about other ways to give people that exposure. I was fortunate in the role that I was in, and I wanted to look at how we could apply those learnings.

I started work on the idea in 2019, through a conversation with my mentor. The 30% Club has a cross-sector mentoring programme, and that perspective both through the lens of another generation and another industry was really valuable.[12] We were talking about career paths, and in my role, it was one that did not flow up to the board. That prompted a discussion around how we change career paths and provide better access to the board.

That led me to research what was happening at other companies. The BBC under 30 project was one. Santander's Millennial Board was another – a board born out of reverse mentoring. In a newsroom environment, it was important to draw on examples from the media industry and beyond, and I ended up with what I saw as the best of combination of other approaches for the best purposes of the FT. Looking at what was happening in different industries was a huge influence – confirming the hunch that so often we feel we are unique in our areas, but it's not unique when it comes to talent development.

I workshopped the plan up through the organisation into a governance review that was taking place, and from there we got the green light. The vision was to create a diverse group of high potential leaders, exchanging ideas and forging strong connections, providing fresh perspective on the FT strategy – and making it a more collaborative, inclusive place to work.

As I reflect on it, where it really began was with more of a founding question – what would happen if we selected a board of upcoming leaders that was as diverse as possible?

How does the multigenerational workplace manifest at the FT?

We're a large organisation with employees from all kinds of backgrounds, disciplines and locations. The age distribution of the FT's global staff is around 22% aged 29 or under, 39% aged between 30 and 39, 22% aged between 40 and 49 and 17% aged 50 or over.[13] In the Editorial Department, we have journalists who have been in the newsroom for decades – some of them have been at the FT for their entire careers, working alongside people early in their careers. And early career hiring is really important to us. Every year we publish a DE&I report, and our latest report shows a record number of young people from diverse backgrounds who participated in one of our early career programmes – including the NGB.

> **"Working alongside people from other departments and teams helped us to break down some of those silos that can exist in companies."**
>
> Elizabeth Pears, Member of the NGB 2022 cohort[14]

As we connect this into the FT's strategic ambitions, what are the key challenges – and opportunities – that the FT is solving for?

It's a really competitive landscape for talent, so showcasing all the work and the programmes at the FT is key. For example, Glassdoor, which is determined on anonymous employee feedback, has named the FT among the best places to work in the UK. That's the challenge – how do we break through to attract and reach the best talent in every department, across commercial, marketing and tech, as well as editorial. The most successful projects always involve collaboration across the departments. This is why we want to hear what the NGB members care about and why – looking at how that overlaps with what the board wants, and the business needs and where we channel our energy.

You are now in the fourth cohort of the NGB. What is the remit of the current cohort, and how has influence and impact evolved as the NGB evolves?

The NGB's remit is to participate in cross-departmental discussions, offer feedback and provide a fresh perspective on our strategy to benefit the company as a whole and achieve the objectives of the programme. All individuals in the NGB will be paired in working partnerships with a member of the FT Group management board. The working partnerships are a useful way to encourage open conversations, often leading to a far greater appreciation of the challenges faced by our employees.

The NGB is always a forward-looking, solutions-focused group and a source of rapid, diverse and trusted feedback and ideas from the wider business. It isn't output focused – its value lies in being a real-time channel for perspectives and ideas. In that spirit, the NGB is an advisory body rather than one that holds decision-making power. As one of the NGB members has said: *"When you hear a board member use your words – that's special."*

Consistent themes have emerged across the cohorts – DEI and silo-busting, which goes back to the strategic importance of collaboration, and adapting around a post-pandemic world. There is huge value in the NGB acting as ears on the ground. Are our people understanding what's happening with big ticket projects and moves? There's a role that the NGB play in feeding that up to the board. Reflecting that pulse of communications, surfacing the things that are really on people's minds, and what we need to index on.

The NGB organically organised itself into three work-streams for every cohort, but the members are not restricted to that. With most cohorts, there has been chop and change across the workstreams, so people have more exposure. The big learning has been creating the room to be responsive. The whole idea is for the NGB to be responsive in a useful way – you want to avoid being overly prescriptive with their time. We learned to give them the wiggle room to organically evolve.

The first cohort created a lot of projects, and we learned from that to evolve it to be much more of an advisory board. Within each cohort's one-year tenure, what we learned was that their real power lies in giving that real-time feedback. As I think about the things that they have influenced, I'll share the ones that I'm most proud of.

The development of the FT's environmental sustainability strategy is one, where they wrote the aim, objectives and measures. This was through collaboration with many others in the business, and with board members bought in. And the impact is still rolling out. Another is improvements to the paid leave policy for women and parents, which NGB members worked on in collaboration with FT Women. FT Women is one of our many Employee Resource Groups (ERGs) across the business, where members contribute alongside their day job. I think the reason why the ERGs succeed at the FT is because they started as grass-roots organisations – none of it is top down. They came about through colleagues getting together because they care about something and want to contribute. The NGB went on to play a role in the FT establishing extended leave for ERG members, which was about recognising their time and contribution. FT Collaborate is another good example – a mini secondment scheme which builds capacity for one-off projects through an open-sourced platform. Again, the connectivity that has happened between people as a result is a really positive consequence.

Silo busting is important for us in terms of how we operate more effectively at the FT, and a favourite of mine that the NGB influenced is a 'management peer support' scheme – where we pair managers across departments. People may have completely different roles, but their management experience has a lot of cross-over, so this became a good example of how we can learn more from our peers in different roles, but through shared experiences.

My big measure of success for the NGB is the board members making the time, and in getting to do another cohort. That means if it's having a positive influence, it's worth the effort.

When we talk about Next Generation Boards in a corporate context, they tend to index on creating a purposeful lens through a specific generation, or younger generations. At the FT you have a different definition. And I'd like to open that up, as it may inspire other organisations who want to implement the platform, but not limit it by age.

That's right. It's called 'next generation' not by age, but by definition of the upcoming generation of talent of the FT Board. It's also 'next gen' in the sense of what's ahead, as we think as a business about what's coming next. In the application process, we ask candidates three questions which test for thinking beyond themselves, beyond their department, and ideally up to company level, or beyond and where we sit within the industry. So it's high potential talent. We have a selection committee that shortlists the applications blind, and from there we select on the diversity of the group, also factoring their potential for collaboration. Our NGB's composition has been across Gen Z, Millennial and Gen X upcoming leaders as the most diverse group that we can create. The goal is to maximise diversity of thought.

What is key to success in terms of operationalising the NGB? The biggest lesson? And the biggest piece of advice that you would give to someone else?

The biggest lesson is to give yourself room, for the NGB to be responsive. For every cohort the most value they have brought has been around a major event that we couldn't have planned for – as we saw through the pandemic and the rapid rise of AI. The NGB was able to constructively feed advice to the senior board and influence the way policies were shared with the company. My biggest piece of advice for anyone setting up a next generation board is to have a dedicated project manager. They need to be a separate force that can jump between the groups and play the connector role – someone empowered, trusted and with capacity to be the guardrails for questions and ideas coming out of the group.

What does the legacy look like?

On the project side, the lasting projects that have a positive impact on the FT are the ones that go beyond the tenure of each cohort. It's about their ongoing influence as an advisory group – with long-term impact. One of the most valuable things to come from the NGB is listening sessions. It was the first cohort who created structure for listening sessions with staff on any given topic – from policy to a big news event. It made it easier for everyone around the company to have a chance to be heard, up to board level, in a constructive setting.

On the professional growth and career pathway front, I go back to my vision – giving more people access to the information and connections I had. As it's in its fourth cohort, we now have a growing group of Alumni who have forged really deep relationships. It's an important horizontal connection and peer group that will influence how they operate and mentor people going forward. It's about connecting people up – and how they continue to pass it on.

Platform:	Next Generation Board
Geography:	Global
Industries:	Media
Launched:	2020
Purpose:	To provide a fresh perspective on the FT strategy
Composition:	Open to FT upcoming leaders (no age restriction)
Members:	10
Tenure:	12 months
Alumni:	Fourth cohort

LIBERTY GLOBAL

Entrepreneurial energy

Schiphol-Rijk, The Netherlands

Liberty Global is a world leader in broadband, video and mobile communications, with headquarters in Denver, London and Amsterdam. Brands in its portfolio include Virgin Media 02 in the UK, VodafoneZiggo in the Netherlands, Telenet in Belgium and Sunrise in Switzerland, with its investment arm, Liberty Global Ventures, invested in infrastructure, technology and content brands, such as Atlas Edge data centres and the Formula E racing series. In 2023, they made another investment, also marking a first for the company in establishing The Liberty Global Youth Council. We spoke with **Agata Ulicka, Director Diversity, Equity and Inclusion, and champion of the Youth Council, Soraya Loerts, Chief DEI Officer, MD Talent & Belonging, and inaugural Youth Council members Liv Conroy-Smith and Arnie Nederpel.**

Could you set the wider context of the workplace at liberty global for us?

Agata: "Liberty Global operates in many countries which gives us the opportunity to learn from each other. As brands, we share a similar approach to the multigenerational workforce. We are diverse in terms of the model, with multiple programmes and strategies, which include Graduate Schemes; Employee Resource Groups (ERGs); Upskilling and leadership training; Social impact and volunteering, and we advocate for cross-group mobility."

"The Youth Council was formalised as an independent voice of appointed members, sponsored by the CEO, and meets regularly with the Executive Leadership Team. Harnessing the thinking and culture of next generations to lead to greater diversity of thought and perspectives was important, as the Youth Council serves as a space for testing new ideas, and activating and accelerating initiatives with relevance to consumers, investors, employees, and policymakers."

Liv: "The commitment to The Youth Council sent an important message about the ambition to innovate the business, our way of working, and about openness to different perspectives."

"It signalled the willingness to evolve and challenge the status quo – joining The Youth Council was a chance to be part of getting more involved in that positive change."

One of the values of Liberty Global is "United – We collaborate and embrace our differences to achieve our goals." With that in mind, can you share with us the wider context behind Liberty Global's commitment to establishing a next generation board?

Agata: "Closing the gap between management and younger generations was important to us at a time when Gen Z is not just entering the workforce but also becoming a powerhouse in the consumer market. We had three pillars that informed it: 1. The changing market conditions and the role of technology and innovation; 2. The Future of work post-pandemic – establishing more clarity around how we build the culture, and the practical changes and 3. Sustainability – we know Gen Z and younger Millennials grew up with this 'crisis anxiety', and sustainability is a big part of that. We saw The Youth Council as a central part of our employer brand proposition as we are fighting for the best talent and looking to future proof our organisation on all these fronts."

"As I have been reflecting on it, the entrepreneurial spirit of The Youth Council is also testament to our foundations. Liberty Global has a leading role in shaping our industry. Our company has constantly reinvented itself reacting to the opportunities and changes in the markets. It's that DNA that we're building on."

Arnie: "What was motivating for me was the level of buy-in from the business and the executive leadership team. The announcement that the company was making this commitment in this type of platform was a key signal to me."

Liv: "Subject matter expertise is something that is really valued within our organisation – with people who have a wealth of knowledge and expertise. As a generation that has grown up with and through the digital transformation, we have different lenses, which gives us a generational subject matter expertise. I saw the Youth Council opportunity as giving us more agency around the meeting of those skillsets."

> "Innovation needs psychological safety
> in order to thrive."

As we connect the strategic ambition with the multigenerational workplace, what are the key challenges – and opportunities – that Liberty Global is solving for?

Agata: "Our continued commitment to DE&I is a key priority. Space for innovation and sharing ideas that are unconventional is key in striking new relevance with new generations of consumers and employees. So, looking at how we become more relevant for young generations. As we are thinking about the changing employee needs combined with the demand to expand our talent pipeline, we are adopting new ways of acquiring and nurturing talent, and we double down on looking for talent in somewhat unexpected places. Therefore investing in upskilling and mobility for your current talent becomes all the more important. Again, this is where The Youth Council sends a signal of how much this matters to us and of the ways in which we are investing. What is important to all of this is making leadership accessible for everyone. Innovation needs psychological safety in order to thrive, and we want everyone to be able to speak up and to listen to other perspectives and ideas."

Soraya: "At Liberty, diversity of thought, combined with our strong commitment to inclusion, is the cornerstone to drive innovation and high performance. Embracing and amplifying the voice of our younger workforce through our newly formed Youth Council plays an indispensable role in all of this. Attracting the best talent and fostering a culture of belonging and dynamic thinking is essential for any business to thrive in today's competitive landscape. We are in our first year and cohort of the Youth Council, and I can already feel the energy that they bring and see the impact they are making."

The Youth Council is in its founding year – how is it working in practical terms, and what does operationalisation look like? How do you balance the democracy with accountability?

Arnie: "We have shared ambitions around what matters to us, and what we want to contribute to in technology, sustainability and the future of work. One challenge that we have been working through in practical terms, is our role as The Youth Council, whether we are a sounding board or a change agent, or where and when we might be both."

Agata: "What we find inspiring about The Youth Council is their ability to connect into existing plans in the organisation as they provide their unique perspectives – with that we challenge our own thinking for a greater impact for all. What we can envision coming out of this is greater acceleration on action, and better integration of work that is underway. Within the three pillars that we talked about, the Youth Council's discussions are focused both within and outside the business. Their outside focus is on customer experience, while the discussions that they're having around the employee experience are on the future of work, specifically building culture and connections in hybrid working and workplace optimisation in a wider sense – looking at real collaboration and how we thrive at work. With their work on sustainability, one of the motivations that we have seen and heard is how intangible it can feel to create an impact on the triple bottom line.

A question that The Youth Council is engaging with is what practical change they can begin with – as a result they are looking at customer experience, sustainable travel policies, the future of work and future talent strategy."

Liv: "We have learned a lot already about how systems can help in taking ownership of what we want to achieve. At the beginning of our tenure, we all wanted to be as agile as possible, but we have learned through the first months of our tenure that there is a reason why systems work, particularly in a professional environment."

If you had a wish for the youth council, what would it be?

Arnie: "We want to have contributed to something that everyone can recognise the Youth Council for having inspired. And something that we can be proud of."

Liv: "We recognise that being the founding cohort is a unique role and responsibility, so this is also about planting the seeds for the next cohort – and if we had the first mandate, we are enabling them to have the full mandate."

Agata: "What I am most passionate about is the future direction of the business and human potential – and the point of connection. This is where our commitment in The Youth Council has a role to play, and I see it coming into play even more on how we translate action at scale. Our Youth Council is proof of Liberty's entrepreneurial, unlimited spirit, propelling us toward a progressive and inclusive future."

FAST FACTS

LIBERTY GLOBAL

Platform:	Next Generation Board
Geography:	Global
Industries:	Telecommunications
Launched:	2023
Purpose:	Harnessing next generation and youth insights and culture into the business, leading to a greater diversity of thought
Composition:	Open to Liberty Global employees aged up to 35 years
Members:	12
Tenure:	12–18 months

"Old power works like a currency. It is held by few. New power operates . . . like a current. It is made by many . . . open, participatory, and peer-driven. It uploads, and it distributes."

Jeremy Heimans and Henry Timms

This incisive set of tensions is posited in *Understanding new Power*, published in the *Harvard Business Review*. The metaphor shift from "currency" to "current" sets up the energy that we want to pass on to you in this chapter, inspired by work that is "open, participatory and driven" across generations, uploading and distributing that energy into business and society.

7

Intergenerational Alliances

The words *"Intergenerational"* and *"Alliance"* are packed with meaning and possibilities. The very lack of a single definition of these alliances is something that we found all the more inspiring in the context of the multiple and interrelated challenges faced at work in the flux of our times. Throughout the book, collaboration has been central to the range of organisations that we have spoken with. In this chapter we deep dive into Intergenerational Alliances in their many forms, through different types of collaborations, coalitions and partnerships.

Exploring their intention and manifestations, on a very practical level, we unpack how the benefits can be achieved and the challenges overcome, especially in evolving contexts. We take a deeper look at a spectrum of intergenerational alliances which stand out in terms of their ambition and success – from the partnership between the United Nations Development Programme (UNDP) and Korean-based global technology giant Samsung, the work and systems ecosystems of Imaginable Futures in Africa, the matrixed ecosystems of the EU Commission and Parliament, and the pioneering multidimensional platform of the St Gallen Symposium.

Intergenerational alliances are at the very intersection of things and are at the heart of arriving at a more positive and productive place for all generations at work. Moreover, it is through stimulating more intergenerational thinking and ways of working that we will realise the solutions to address the complexity of challenges in the world today as well as create extraordinary opportunities that have yet to be imagined.

What do we mean by an intergenerational alliance?

Whether expressed through *"partnerships"*, *"collaborations"*, *"coalitions"* or other forms and framing, intergenerational alliances can take different forms, and many use the terms interchangeably through different cultures and contexts. Our focus is on the *intent* and in identifying progressive thinking and successful models in different contexts *and on their respective and collective impact*.

At its essence, an intergenerational alliance is a relationship between a number of generations which has been formed for mutual benefit. It may be formal or informal or a mix of the two. It may be within a single organisation or between a number of organisations of the same or different types. It may develop organically and informally or intentionally with more structure and process, and by its very nature, will continue to adapt.

The UNDP-Samsung partnership is a powerful example of a public-private partnership which, at its heart, is an intergenerational alliance, resulting in over 300 million Galaxy devices used by people of all ages having the global Goals app. The purpose is to raise awareness across societies in the Sustainable Development Goals (SDGs), providing a highly accessible way to connect people across generations with opportunities to engage around the Goals. The fact that the UNDP and Samsung saw the potential

> **"What is most powerful about these collaborations is their capacity to capture and catalyse mindset change."**
>
> Zubair Junjunia

for progress through engaging young leaders through the app and its communications has been acknowledged as a key success factor. Named after the number of the SDGs, 'Generation17' was created in 2020 as a platform and community of young leaders across the world.

As Nadine Khaouli, a Generation17 Leader and Youth Engagement Coordinator at the UNDP states: *"The value of the partnership is in multiplying the effect. The main function is to raise awareness, connection and a call to action around the SDGs, where people can contribute and engage. And by supporting the Generation17 Young Leaders, the aim is to empower them as a community, elevate their voices and amplify their impact, also leveraging The UN General Assembly forum, the ECOSOC Youth Forum, Samsung Unpacked events and other speaking and networking opportunities. It's very much about collaboration. Many young activists and leaders don't engage on competitive terms. It's more about mentorship and seeking to understand. We are all working on shared goals, but we're doing it through different ways, contexts and challenges. Because our experiences are different, you get inspired by the work of others. We all have a learning mindset. We like to learn from each other."*

Zubair Junjunia, a Generation17 leader and Founder of ZNotes continues: *"The origin story behind the platform is interesting, in itself, because of how it was constructed. There was a clear vision and strategy when it was first set up in 2020, but intentionally without a lot of prescriptive structure, as the idea was to construct it in partnership with young people. As I joined this group, what I found most inspiring was the collective knowledge built across geographies and problem spaces but aligned on the fundamental belief of creating a fair, just and prosperous world."*

Discussing the outcomes of the alliance, Zubair affords a refreshing perspective on how we think about measurement in more lateral terms: *"The value of peer community and connections through this alliance is immeasurable. There are many ways to consider and measure impact, but one that I found useful is the taxonomy of three: When I reflect on impact taxonomies with other founders and investors, I tend to land on three: one is 'impact out', which is scale; another is influence, or what is described as 'impact up'; and the third is 'impact deep', which is about changing mindsets. Each of these happens at a different scale, but a successful intervention encapsulates all three."*

"What is most powerful about these collaborations is their capacity to capture and catalyse mindset change. With Generation17, each young leader has an incredible influence and collectively reaches tens of millions of people around the world. The collective knowledge of this group, combined with the opportunities we make available to our respective communities to participate and contribute means that we are more likely to see a continual nudge effect in how we all contribute to society. This is about expanding our lenses on what we value and stretching our capacity to add value through greater influence and impact. Measuring the benefits of mindset shifts through values and how people interact through more generous

behaviours and more collaborative ways of working is much harder, but it's a ripple effect that is very real."

In a similar way in the UK, 'The Big Help Out' is an intergenerational alliance which also consists of a large number of partnerships between public services, businesses and civil society organisations, across the country. It was founded by the Royal Voluntary Service and other leading charities including the Scouts and mobilised over 7.2 million people in 2023 including 2000 businesses to support 35,000 voluntary organisations to increase their social impact. It works through a mix of formal agreements and informal understandings together with mass mobilisation on a local and very specific basis. Demographic statistics from a sample of over 4200 of the volunteers taking part showed a fascinating split by age: 18–25 (25%); 25–34 (20%); 35–45 (13%); 45–54 (6%); 55–64 (4%); 65–74 (5%); 75+ (7%). With over 80% of people taking part meeting someone from a different background, it stimulated greater appreciation of different generations and the challenges they face as well as changed many perceptions of each other about older and younger groups.

> **"Intergenerational issues are not a zero-sum game. The truth is that the greatest potential lies in combining the strengths of all age groups to create value that is greater than the sum of its parts."**
>
> Megan Hippo, Stellenbosch University, South Africa, St Gallen Symposium Leader of Tomorrow

The essential benefit of an intergenerational alliance can be summed up in the most powerful and simple terms: *"Better*

Together". As to why we are better together, the typical reasons given span the following:

- Enhancing employment propositions, engagement, motivation and retention
- Increased innovation and creativity
- Stronger levels of organisational cohesiveness and resilience
- Greater constructive challenge at many and sometimes all parts and levels of the organisation
- Enhanced legitimacy with stakeholder groups
- Stronger diversity and inclusiveness

Through combining knowledge, perspectives, skills and resources through mutually supportive actions, we are more likely to achieve our common purpose. Dov Seidman, the Founder and Executive Chairman of The HOW Institute for Society, speaks to this in the character and capabilities that we will need to build on through the context of our times: *"our creativity, our curiosity and, at our best, our capacity for hope, ethics, empathy, grit and collaborating with others."*[1] Through our research, experience and as evidenced through other bodies of work,[2] the better generations understand each other, the greater the creativity, the healthier the tensions and the higher the quality of decisions and engagement to execute them.

The power gained from mobilising diverse groups of people is far greater than we can deliver either on our own or in a small group drawn from a single generation. Having the right mindset, defining and setting that North Star, and the culture and communications to support it, are vital to generating this power. The Mars company's principles and the use of their Compass, as described in the Family Businesses chapter, are useful frameworks to help achieve this. The principles of Mutuality, Freedom and Responsibility are especially apposite.

Mutuality which works across all stakeholder groups and generations within and outside the business, is summed up as follows: "Mutuality is a belief with powerful implications. It recognizes that we benefit when others gain too and compels us to think about others' interests as well as our own. Creating enduring, shared benefits has been part of our success for more than a century."

Freedom makes specific mention of generations: "Our financial freedom means we can think across generations, not quarters. It enables us to make choices that balance the needs of today with our aspirations for tomorrow."

Responsibility is framed as: "We take responsibility without being asked. We support the responsibilities of others." In talking with Victoria Mars, "without being asked" stood out, because it was driven by the right thing to do for the wider collective.

The St Gallen Symposium, profiled in this chapter, is one of the world's leading platforms for cross-generational dialogue on economic, political and social development. As you will see, it has been a constant source of creativity and a proactive collaborator. Its collaboration with The Club of Rome (created in 1968 to address the multiple crises facing humanity and the planet), to create a New

Generational Contract is all the more thought provoking through the practicality underpinning its potential.

As is so often the case, the why is easier than the how. The cases and conversations that we feature in this chapter have been selected to show the many practical ways in which intergenerational alliances can be created and operated successfully. Success is the result of organisations that have a learning mindset at their core. If you are considering whether to create an intergenerational alliance and how to develop it, being transparent about potential challenges will minimise the risk of them occurring. The 'learn-it-all' organisations (to quote Satya Nadella), use the insights from the challenges they encounter to constantly inform the ongoing and future success of the alliance.

What we found through our research was often a common set of challenges, frustrations and pitfalls, which we share below.

- Lack of board and leadership team commitment.
- Unrealistic expectations.
- A lack of clarity and focus of purpose.
- Trying to do too many things.
- Poor execution of fundamentally sound ideas.
- Weak communication.
- Giving up too early when there are teething issues.
- Stimulating challenge and change and then being surprised by challenge and desire for change.

A prerequisite for an intergenerational alliance, as with any other form, is both clarity and alignment of purpose and a conviction that life will be better with one rather than without. For example, the desire to have an input and a voice in decision-making is a purpose cited frequently by younger generations as a driver for an intergenerational alliance. For the organisation this is often matched by the need to make more informed decisions and achieve higher levels of engagement in delivering them. We can gain different things from a common collaborative activity.

> *"Intergenerational networks have emerged as another practical approach to turning generational difference into both cultural and competitive advantage."*

As part of advancing the wider mission of more effective and productive intergenerational dialogue, there is often work taking place specific to a given generation. Where companies do this well is in how they recognise and communicate it as part of the business strategy, and wider intergenerational thinking across their organisation. As we have seen, Next Generation Boards tend to be formed from within a generation or two adjacent generations, and their purpose wired into the long-term business strategy.

The determining factor is how these commitments relate to the entire organisation. Gucci's shadow board, for example, was related to their Culture of Purpose and driven by the need for organisational transformation and the desire to better connect with next generations of customers and employees. If that is the driver, then understanding what those customers and employees want and need, and how to engage them, underpins the right strategy.

Intergenerational networks have emerged as another practical approach to turning generational difference into both cultural and competitive advantage. The financial industry is one that has seen a rise in these commitments, from brands such as Bank of America, HSBC and Standard Chartered. As Standard Chartered says: *"As we see changes in our workforce and client demographic through generational diversity, it's important for us to leverage generational differences and work together to bridge gaps so everyone feels valued and that they can contribute to our purpose. We want to leverage generational experiences to increase innovation and deliver products and services for colleagues and clients at various life stages."*[3]

Skills transfer programmes are also being used to retain core capabilities. For example, BMW's Senior Experts programme[4] has a very clear purpose with retired workers returning to the company part-time to share their expertise with younger colleagues in order to preserve critical capabilities and reenergise it through the business.

Turning generational difference into a strength was Bank of America's objective in developing a training programme and ongoing education for employees about the value of multigenerational teams and age inclusion. Their Inter-Generational Employee Network was designed to create opportunities for networking, development and mentoring across all generations. Adobe, Cisco and Salesforce are some of the leading brands that have invested in specific support for those with elderly care commitments and responsibilities. Emily McCrary-Ruiz-Esparza speaks to the wider context of up to eight generations living in the United States: *"as longevity continues to soar, nine or ten generations may end up living together before mid-century.*"[5] SentinelOne, a cybersecurity firm based in California, is one company that has set its own standard in family leave, expanding their parental leave policies to include grandparents. As McCrary-Ruiz-Esparza continues: "*The need for multigenerational family care is likely to grow, especially because many grandparents are already handling both work and care. According to the US Census Bureau, there are more than 7 million grandparents living with grandchildren who are under age 18, and about half of those grandparents are in the workforce.*" One way to look at developing a strategy for an intergenerational alliance is to undertake a classic stakeholder analysis where each generation is viewed as a stakeholder group.

A stakeholder analysis tool that we find both relevant and resonant in this context, is that pioneered at Cranfield University by Professor Andy Neely, Chris Adams and Mike Kennerley, and described in their book *The Performance Prism*.[6] What is so useful about this technique is its clarity and practicality, and the agility with which you can develop a robust and adaptable strategy for maximising the shared value between stakeholders:

- Start by being clear about what you mean by a stakeholder. A good definition is Edward Freeman's "Anyone who affects or is affected by the organisation".[7]
- Decide who your most important five or six stakeholder groups are. For example, customers, staff, suppliers, beneficiaries, funders, etc.
- Work out and state in one summary sentence what each stakeholder group wants and needs from you (The SWANS: Stakeholder Wants and Needs).

- Do the same for what the organisation wants from each and needs from each stakeholder group (The OWANS: Our Wants and Needs)
- Get the metrics and data in place to measure whether stakeholders are getting what they want and need, and whether you are getting what you want and need from them.
- It is usually clear then what the strategy for each stakeholder group should be, and as importantly what an integrated strategy should be, which balances our needs and theirs as well as the needs and wants of different groups.

It is a straightforward, but powerful approach to take when devising an intergenerational strategy – working out what each generational group wants and needs from the organisation, as well as what the organisation wants and needs of them. The strategy should naturally flow and evolve as you figure out ways to maximise and to balance the various needs and wants of different generations.

What we measure, how we measure it and why

Historically, many have relied upon traditional customer and staff engagement surveys and have not used the extensive amount of other data that their organisations already hold. In using these traditional techniques not all have focused on what people *do* as well as what they *say*.

Understanding what people do and how they really feel as well as what they say is vitally important, whether looking at different churn rates by generation, analysing exit interviews as well as understanding the strongest motivational factors, which may differ by generation. As we look to investment in learning, development and skills training, cohort-specific approaches remain important, but increasingly the need and opportunity is in the 'diagonals', bringing people together across disciplines and tenures. Providing coaching and mentoring opportunities tended to be focused on younger groups when this is something valuable throughout careers, and being trained to coach or mentor is valuable at all stages. Mutual mentoring is one of the approaches, from our research, that seems to be gaining more traction and resulting in more intrinsic benefit.

Having relevant, straightforward metrics and data that can be intelligently integrated, providing better transparency and real-time insight is critical to success in working out where to maximise the time or money spent as well as to continuously learn and adapt. What is wanted and needed by an organisation, and by individuals, changes. Spotting these trends early can be highly valuable.

We would agree with the Organisation for Economic Co-operation and Development (OECD) that there is significant potential for Human Resource Systems to deliver more in this area. *"One area in which progress has been lacking so far are human resource performance systems. These need to better capture the collective impact of an age-diverse and – inclusive workforce . . . much of the benefits of age diversity comes from spillovers or the mix of ages, with employees collaborating and complementing and learning from each other. Yet, current human resource systems fall short in two ways: they tend to incentivise individual contributions rather than capturing the productivity and collective impact of an age-diverse workforce;*

and they might even stifle productivity by discouraging collaboration, while encouraging internal competition."[8]

The advent of Artificial Intelligence alongside the rise of big data and analytics combined with increasingly sophisticated data visualisation techniques means that it is becoming more practical and affordable. The prize is considerable, but there are also risks in terms of employee data privacy and the way that it is used. There are big differences in the way that some are using such data, from the hugely positive to the more 'Orwellian' monitoring cultures.

Striking the right balance on this and in maximising the benefit of intergenerational alliances means that development and training of those leading them is crucial irrespective of age or position. As is ensuring that there are good processes for feedback and review, which are both agile and capable of being continuously adapted. The employers who genuinely want to maximise the value of five generations at work are not only indexing on training their leaders and their entry-level colleagues. They think hard about continuous development at all stages of progression and age. As Stefano Scarpetta, Director of Employment, Labour and Social Affairs at the OECD states in the American Association of Retired Persons (AARP) "Promoting an Age-inclusive Workforce" report: *"If employers and other key stakeholders are to adapt to ongoing changes in the world of work — now accelerated by the COVID-19 pandemic — they will need to reevaluate their policies and practices with an eye toward an age-inclusive workforce."*

In an innovative intergenerational alliance, three organisations have come together to open-source a range of resources and tools to encourage and make it easier for other organisations to make progress on their multigenerational agendas. The platform Growing with Age is the result of a collaboration between AARP, OECD and the World Economic Forum (WEF). Recognised in Fast Company's annual global innovation awards, the platform has over 100 brand partners, across companies such as Allianz, Amgen, Bank of America, Johnson & Johnson, SAP and The New York Times.

"Better decisions, Innovation and Authenticity"

The purpose of social impact investor Imaginable Futures' intergenerational alliance is *"Better decisions, Innovation and Authenticity"*. As we will see in the conversation in this chapter, they have invested in over 30 not- and for-profit organisations in Africa. They acknowledge the complexity of education systems in the countries in which they operate, and that part of this complexity is the interdependencies at play between the stakeholders involved across generations. By way of example, the "Theory of Change" for Kenyan education illustrates how critical they see systems thinking to their success not just to hear the voices of many generations, but to listen to them with care, to enable those voices to hear other voices and to devise sustainable solutions.[9]

Intergenerational alliances are also at the heart of moving on from what we see as the current divisive discourse to a more productive and positive place. Finding context-specific ways to stimulate generations working together, supporting each other and combining their different talents, experiences and perspectives has enormous potential as we have seen already. What we found through our research was a range of practical solutions to some of the common challenges that we identified earlier, and which are further evidenced in the conversations to follow. What we go on to unpack through multigenerational conversations with the EU Commission and Parliament, Imaginable Futures (IF) and the St Gallen Symposium is a series of progressive, long-term thinking inspiring practical solutions and ongoing innovation.

Problem: Lack of stakeholder engagement.

Solution: Set up systems that rely on interdependence to create more effective stakeholder engagement and commitment – as evidenced in IF's work in community engagement through a shared vision of education and interdependence between schools and communities.

Problem: Unrealistic expectations; A lack of clarity and focus of purpose.

Solution: Instead of starting too big, develop in stages, such as pilot and learning phases, before rolling out larger initiatives. IF was intentional in how it established its Youth Advisory Board – starting small where its core African team is based in Kenya and constructing the first five months as a pilot and learning phase.

Problem: Trying to do too many things; poor execution of fundamentally sound ideas.

Solution: The EU Commission and Parliament's investment in the Schuman recruitment and development programme has shown the power of creating a talent magnet across the institutions that thrives through continual investment and renewal.

Problem: Stimulating challenge and change and then being surprised by challenge and desire for change.

Solution: Challenge is actively invited by St Gallen through a series and cycle of programmes and used to inform its year-round work. Setting expectations is vital, and something that St Gallen excels in, also enabling a culture where surprises are seized on as opportunities.

The organisations that you will hear from in the conversations to follow are working on a global scale with intergenerational groups on large social issues. The different ways in which they achieve it, from grass-roots work in communities, to complex, matrixed organisations, offer insights in lessons across mindset, skillset and toolkit that have relevance for us all. In conversation across cultures and generations, we hope that they will inspire you.

IMAGINABLE FUTURES

Invest for Success as Good Ancestors

Nairobi

Imaginable Futures (IF), a venture of The Omidyar Group, is a social change funder supporting people, ideas and initiatives that contribute to more equitable and healthy systems so that all learners, families and communities can thrive. Investing at the intersection of learning and equity, IF collaborates with communities and partners to disrupt patterns of inequity and catalyse meaningful change for learners of all ages in Brazil, Sub-Saharan Africa and the United States. At the time of writing, it had invested more than $300m alongside over 200 portfolio partners in over 50 countries.

There are a number of points of distinction in the IF approach which contribute to their effectiveness in working across generations to achieve the impact they are seeking. The first relates to the contexts they operate in and the fact that in their view *"Far too many places around the world are rooted in systems built on – and still rampant with – racism and other forms of injustice,"*[10] The second is the systems thinking approach they take in all that they do which *"Allows us to better understand these complex environments beyond just treating the symptoms to address intractable social problems, so that everyone, not just a privileged few can thrive."* Adding explicitly that: *"Our aspirations for impact require us to be both courageous and humble in engaging complex systems. A systems approach is both a concept we use to inform our strategies and a practice we use to do our daily work."*

Diversity of generations, and generations to come, are important elements of the system and will continue to be. Therefore finding ways to stimulate intergenerational collaboration is essential both through and with their partners, with their teams and in everyone that they work with. IF are very open about the three core premises through which they operate as a team, and, again, as we see across so many of the cases and conversations, there are common threads:

- Patterns and problems first, tools second;
- Collaboration and 'collective leadership' and
- Learning and Unlearning.

This systems approach and the desire to improve education opportunities and outcomes today, as well as for the next generation is a core part of IF's strategy for their work in Sub-

> **"We believe that unlocking human potential is inherently multigenerational."**[11]

Saharan Africa and was one of the reasons behind the creation and development of the IF Youth Advisory Board (YAB) in Africa. In order to determine the areas in which to invest most effectively, IF has been looking at the root causes and patterns that amplify the socio-economic exclusion of Africa's youth. To aid its understanding of these root causes and patterns, it has placed a high priority on having teams on the ground, in listening and engaging locally with those involved in education systems.

"To have a reorientation in our lives towards future generations and leaving things better than we found them was really powerful for us."

Amongst many things, including its many partnerships across the region with organisations of many types across the public, private and civil society spectra, this approach inspired the formation of the YAB in late 2021 with the aim of shaping its work and its investment strategy. The belief was that developing strong connections with young people would create effective feedback loops from those most in need of, and those most impacted by, its work, as well as providing proximity and legitimacy with and for the communities in which it works. The stated aims of the YAB remain those at the outset, namely to:

- Foster and deepen authentic connections among young people and provide opportunities to build their social capital.
- Create spaces for learning, growth and harnessing their power in tackling issues pertinent to them and their communities.
- Play an advisory role in the work of IF, supporting us to advance youth-centric perspectives and building together with them as trusted thought partners.

Speaking with YAB member Pamela Omondi, the founder of the Gift with Love Foundation, which empowers girls and young women through menstrual health and hygiene education and mentorship, we gained a deeper insight into what this meant in real terms: *"It became much more for*

us. We became aware of the concept of The Good Ances-
tor from the philosopher Roman Krznaric's book of the
same name. To have a reorientation in our lives towards
future generations and leaving things better than we found
them was really powerful for us."

As Roman Krznaric puts it more dramatically, *"future*
generations aren't here to challenge this pillaging of their
inheritance'. '. . . the great silent majority of future genera-
tions is rendered powerless. Yet we can influence on their
behalf, and we should. We must."

This proved a powerful motivation when combined with
what Teresa Mbagaya, Principal at Imaginable Futures,
describes as: *"The three pillars upon which YAB depends:*
Trust, Growth and Proximity." One of the distinguish-
ing features of IF's YAB is the degree of investment in the
development of the board members. This goes beyond
skills training and includes a mentorship and coaching
programme. It has also involved YAB members as informal advisers on new IF investments within Africa, which
has the mutual benefit of exercising their critical thinking and analytical skills at the same time as IF gains fresh
insights on potential investments. To aid inclusivity and
to further demonstrate that their input and time is valued,
alongside the standard expense cover and policy of many
Youth Advisory Boards, IF YAB members are also remu-
nerated for their contribution and commitment. IF has
also thought about the different phases of development of
its YAB. It has started small with a Kenyan focus where its
core African team is based and intentionally constructed
the first five months as a pilot and learning phase.

For the IF team, learning has been a constant theme and a route through which the different generations can bond, work together more effectively towards the overall goal as well as gain rich personal development through each other. According to James Mwangi, Founder and Editor of Zinduka, an apolitical youth-centric and culture-shaping platform that seeks to give voice and agency to the youth in Kenya: *"Getting to a place where my voice is being heard and my opinions are being considered has really been the greatest experience here."* As Ashley Jaholo, Founder of Jasiri added: *"Our super-power as young Africans is our adaptability and ability to provide solutions to the problems affecting us."*

Another multi- and intergenerational theme that is strong for IF is their work in Brazil, expanding access through representation. As they put it, "Representation matters. Yet children and young people from historically excluded communities often do not see themselves in leadership positions, undermining real political and decision-making representation. We invest in the career development of values-aligned educators and leaders from black and indigenous communities. We rely on local knowledge to guide our approaches. In this way we're able to help inform public policy decisions and increase stakeholder accountability." All of which embodies the spirit of an intergenerational alliance through public and private and many other partnership lenses.

In Brazil, one of IF's aims has been to foster community through a shared vision of education, and this, by definition, involves all generations and is neither straightforward nor quick to achieve. Yet in their view: "Community engagement in learning inside and outside of school ensures political and collective accountability for quality education. Successful examples illustrate how teachers, administrators and community leaders can showcase how schools are an integral element of overall community outcomes. We support and promote the interdependence between schools and communities and efforts that build a shared vision for learning through a participatory approach."

Speaking with Abdelrahman Hassan at IF, we learned that a lot of the organisations and partners that they work with have also built this kind of learning and listening into their work. Deep listening and partnership with the YAB help to inform what changing norms and mindsets looks like and how that impacts and influences the partners that they work with. As Abdelrahman sums it up: *"You have to invest for success."*

FAST FACTS
IMAGINABLE FUTURES

Platform:	Cross-generational platform, programmes and ecosystem
Geography:	Brazil, Sub-Saharan Africa and the United States
Industries:	Philanthropic Investment
Launched:	2020
Purpose:	To maximise social impact
Composition:	Organisation and network wide

THE ST GALLEN SYMPOSIUM

Lead with the next generation in mind

St Gallen, Switzerland

There are places in the world that sit at a confluence of things. St Gallen is one of them. The St Gallen Symposium is one of the world's leading initiatives for cross-generational dialogue on economic, political and social development. Arriving in St Gallen, there is a sense of awe and wonder that strikes you, with this unique siting and sighting between the mountains, and across the Bodensee, otherwise known as Lake Constance, bordering Germany, Austria and Switzerland. That context and confluence is an apposite emblem of the Symposium, which convenes an eclectic gathering of minds across generations, cultures and industries.

Having worked with the pioneering team at St Gallen, it was a great chance to sit down with **Felix Ruediger, Head of Content and Research,** to unpack the cross-generational trajectory of their work, and to host a conversation across four generations with: **Beat Ulrich, CEO of the St Gallen Symposium; Nadine Merz, an International Students' Committee (ISC) alumna and Head of the 50th ISC; Richard Wäg, Member of the 53rd ISC at the St Gallen Symposium and Sophia Gampp, Head of the 53rd ISC at the St Gallen Symposium.**

St Gallen itself is a storied site of knowledge and knowledge transfer – site of the oldest library in Switzerland and one of the oldest libraries in the world. It is also home to a historical tradition of craft and skills, which seems appropriate for a conversation that will engage with the transfer, exchange and evolution of knowledge across generations. Let us open with how it all began . . .

Felix: "As we look back to the context of 1968 and 1969, these were years of generational tensions with visible unrest on the streets. At a time when conflict defined the relationship between generations, a group of people in St. Gallen took a different approach by coming together to open up a dialogue. It was still very much challenging the status quo, but in a constructive, open and liberal dialogue, that took shape in our first Symposium. This was the beginning of this sustainable and long-term thinking that informs everything that we do today, and that is inherent to cross-generational dialogue – the two core ideas that have always informed the Symposium and its founding. It began with five co-founders, led by Professor Wolfgang Schürer. And it is this same passion of the members that carries it forward today. Schürer tells the story in the publication *Denken und Handeln,* reflecting on engaging their first speakers: *"You grow more from a no than a yes"*. When asked, *"Why are you inviting me?"* Schürer says. *"The answer was, 'We want to learn something from you, and we want you to listen to us.' That was the idea of generational dialogue."*[12]

And what has evolved over time is an ecosystem. The annual Symposium remains at the crux of it, but this is very much a platform and continuum of cross-generational collaboration.

Felix: "As a university, we are already known for having a strong student-initiative culture. And, yes, it is very much an ecosystem, which consists of the annually selected team of around 25 students – the International Students' Committee, and the St Gallen Foundation, who co-create the Symposium, together with alumni. The scale of our ecosystem is really remarkable, including our student alumni body, which is now over 50 years of teams and around 1000 total alumni; our professors; a global network of 300 organisations and business partners; the University itself as our alma mater and hosting institution; our 10,000+ Leaders of Tomorrow alumni, among them around 2000 are under 35; alongside non-profits and think tanks (such as The Club of Rome) and media. Each year at the Symposium we bring together around 1000 cross-generational participants and 100 speakers from 85 nations, among them 200 young entrepreneurs, policymakers and researchers (our "Leaders of Tomorrow") and several hundred senior executives from business and policy."

"Importantly, the work is year-round. The Symposium is a powerful point in the year where we gain better insights, where we are able to pick up many of these ideas and from there we can take some of them forward into impact projects. For example, this is how the New Generational Contract and Young Leaders on Board came about – and we will go on to share more about this work. And I love that many of these alumni come back through the years to support the Symposium. There is a real solidarity there. A lasting solidarity."

"Our turnover in the Symposium's organisational body of 60–70% every year, in line with the student intake and their journey, is also an important part of the ecosystem and how it works, because it's a continuous innovation driver of new ideas, of constructive critique, building constantly into the next level of excellence. It is a masterpiece of organisational learning and memory, continuously handing over to the next generation."

How do you make use of measurement through this evolving ecosystem?

Felix: "It's an interesting point because this is about institutional enablement, and we measure around the value of the Symposium and around our purpose and mission. Our Young Leaders on Board Project, a joint project with Zukunft-Fabrik.2050, has KPIs – we look at how many young leaders we get onto boards. We look at the awareness raised through media publications and events. What's important here is how many of these cross-generational dialogues can have their own magic happening. It's about enabling this cross-generational leadership and learning – some of which we won't be able to keep track of, in a good sense, because this is happening so organically, all over the world. We therefore take a more lateral approach in service of the overall ambition. One of the big measures that we look at is how many intergenerational touchpoints we enable. Our student team alone engages in around 1000 intergenerational meetings a year, plus of course the hundreds, probably thousands of dialogues across the generations that we facilitate at the annual Symposium and our year-round events."

> **"It's like a family business', in which there is a change of generations. Here generations take care of each other: Each new generation knows what the previous generations have achieved, and the previous generations in turn support the new generation with new ideas."**
>
> Maximilian Wörlein, Head of the ISC from 2019 to 2021

"We also make use of this huge network that we have through our Young Leaders on Board project, which seeks to bring young, outstanding experts on the boards of forward-looking organisations. We currently are working with three organisations where we will have young leaders (between 35–40 years) on their boards. One of them is a family business in Germany with around 5000 employees, one an SME in Switzerland, and another is a corporate foundation. Sustainability, in many senses, is a theme across them all. One company is in sustainable architecture and design. Another is a traditional family business looking to better advance a new business model and new way of engaging with customers and clients while being true to its legacy and core business. The third is in mechanical engineering."

Each year there is a theme and call to action around the Symposium. Has that been true since the beginning? And what do those themes tell us over time?

Felix: "The idea was always to have a theme relevant to current developments that enables you to shine a light on a diverse set of issues, while having some academic substance. If we go back through the decades, we see a key interest in the interdependence between corporations and their environmental spheres, including politics, civil society and nature. The foundations of a liberal society were also frequently explored. There are themes looking at the greater role of the organisational practices of management and its function in society. In recent years, we've put an emphasis on themes of sustainability and intergenerational equity – given the many challenges we face today that require us to balance short-term and long-term outlooks.

So, this accumulation of themes around cross-generational dialogue is something that's already relevant, but that will be even more relevant in the long term, with an ageing population and as we need to bring together the present and future more urgently. Therefore, in the context of the intensity of climate change and demographic transitions, the theme for 2024 is 'Confronting Scarcity.'"

As we talk about the importance of language, the 'New Generational Contract' speaks to a joint initiative that you have launched with The Club of Rome.

Felix: "The New Generational Contract is a global impact initiative, guided by seven principles, which we've developed through global intergenerational surveys, hundreds of received student essays and workshops:

1. Responsibility: Considering our Impact Today and Tomorrow
2. Care: Seeing and Supporting each other
3. Voice: Being heard and having a say
4. Collaboration: Joining forces and perspectives
5. Hindsight and Foresight: Looking back to see ahead
6. Regeneration: Revitalising and protecting ecosystems
7. Openness: Striving for a living contract

"Building on these core principles, the initiative seeks to leverage cross-generational leadership and learning for more long-term, regenerative strategies in business and policy. We do this through strategic media work, such as recently in an article in the *Harvard Business Review*, and through dialogues at high-level fora, such as at Building Bridges in Geneva or the SDG Tent in Davos. We also launch concrete projects, that enact the key principles of the NGC, such as our aforementioned Young Leaders on Board project, that exemplifies 'voice', 'collaboration' and 'responsibility' especially."

Partners and partnership, unsurprisingly, are an integral part of advancing the agenda. And it's about a deeper sense of shared value.

Felix: "Partnerships only work when there's a true synergy of values, purpose and mission, which we see across our corporate and non-profit partners. To mention a few of those partners: ABB, Accenture, Boston Consulting Group, The Club of Rome, HCLTech, Omega, Max Schmidheiny Foundation, Swiss Re and The UN SDG Lab. It's about that core convergence, and how we sustain it together. The University of Oxford is a good example of that partnership in The Global Leadership Challenge, which brings together 100 young people every year, co-creating impact projects for the SDGs across generations. And the awareness around this is quite incredible, as we now receive over 2,500 applications for each challenge. As Peter Voser, Chairman ABB Group & Chairman of the St Gallen Symposium's Board of Trustees says, *'Global challenges can only be solved by different generations working together to create a healthier, more prosperous future for everyone.'*"

Reflecting on the work over the years, can you share the stories that stand out for you?

Felix: "This sense of solidarity between the alumni and current student team. This regular engagement that continues with CEOs. It is about these shared mental models and this shared responsibility. I think of a green-tech founder who is now one of the leading actors in the green-tech industry and the role that the Symposium played. I think about Dr. Mamphela Ramphele, until most recently in 2023 Co-President of The Club of Rome, who has visited our offices and the student house several times ahead of the Symposium and energises the students through her stories. I think of one of my ISC colleagues Linn who worked from end to end to get Nicolai Tangen, who leads Norges Bank Investment Management, and the biggest public investor of the world, to come and participate, and to how she conducted the interview with him on stage. I think about Kofi Annan coming to St. Gallen and his quote that greatness doesn't need to come from bigness. I think about the Club of Rome, which first presented its Limits to Growth report at the Symposium in 1972, and how we are now picking it up 50 years later."

"Another special moment for me is 'St Gallen Talks', our joint format with ZEIT ONLINE, where we ask participants five controversial contemporary questions and then have an algorithm match people with different points of view on these questions for cross-generational 1-1 conversations. It is an example of the active mixing and pairing we're doing and that really stands out for people when coming to St Gallen."

> **"The reality is there is no standard. There are a lot of exceptions."**
>
> Sophia Gampp

What are your perspectives and experiences on the challenges and the opportunities for five generations at work?

Nadine: "I think back to my Symposium times, and a lot of challenges come from understanding the other person's perspective and experiences. A colleague once observed that we were working with people who had not been alive when there were key world events, such as 9/11. At the time, I did not think it mattered much. But then I realised that, indeed, they had not experienced what I have. What's important is an understanding of where the other person is coming from. What's important is working in diverse environments. Different perspectives are important to all generations."

Beat: "I refer to our vision, 'lead with the next generation in mind'. I am interested in where the differences are, particularly when it comes to digital transformation, to sustainability. What my generation has grown up with and the way we did business is different. There is a gap, and the discussion around that gap is what we foster as a Symposium."

Sophia: "I really like to work with both the next generations above and below my generation. And it helps you realise and realign your perspective. We are all a step ahead in different ways."

Felix: "You're right, with these big ideas we have to talk about the challenges. It is a constant learning. It needs a willingness from both generations to engage from a professional point of view. Perspective is a powerful point that Nadine reflects on. In the New Generational Contract, we talk about hindsight and foresight – and having the combination of both in what we're doing. If it's done right, this is where things are enabled or realised. We always have the learning and enabling factor in mind. Especially where people are doing it for the first time. There has to be a degree of mutual acceptance. We see this great potential – the energy of young people, the ideas, the strength of us really living this very authentically within our organisation for the purpose and authenticity of the overall cross-generational ambition. For us, living it is so powerful because we have a cross-generational leadership team."

Collaboration has been an operative word since the very beginning. And it's clear that it's taking on new forms. What does effective collaboration look like?

Beat: "It's important to identify the potentials of this cross-generational dialogue. What is the potential when senior leaders and older generations talk with the next generation, as future customers, as employees, etc. This potential and the new ideas that can come out of such a dialogue, we have to describe it even better. And, to your point about how generations are labelled and talked about in unhelpful ways, one of the most important things that we can all do is engage in individual dialogue. This 1-1 dialogue is an important form of collaboration where we really learn."

Richard: "One barrier to collaboration is the willingness to listen. People are willing to talk, but not everyone is willing to listen. Listening is one of the most powerful facilitators of collaboration."

Nadine: "I'm also with Richard, listening goes both ways. I also like your point about unlearning – a lot of companies are doing reverse mentoring, with young generations mentoring established leaders. But I believe the impact of these kind of commitments depends on the culture and the company. It's about making sure it's not a signalling move. I'm also there to learn. It has to go both ways. From the few years that I have been in the workforce, it's much more difficult than I thought. When we think about those quotes by Socrates, Plato and others on the perception of young generations, we realise it's a sentiment that goes back a long way. This is about trying to change something from the roots and whatever you change, we have to have a better understanding together about that vessel for change and what it is that we're actually changing."

"The Symposium is a platform for everyone who is willing to listen and to collaborate. It is also our responsibility to say no. We have had conversations with potential speakers where if we sense that are they interested in their own monologue, we say no. We have to be convinced that this person is with us on our mission."

Felix: "Our alumni and community work is all about collaboration – bringing younger and senior leaders in dialogue with each other. And it's about the empowerment that it enables. For example, we know of many social entrepreneurs who got their first support and push at the Symposium. We have chapters around the world where there is a real sense of purpose-driven involvement, where they continue to connect, and share opportunities. This is about us being part of their journey. And there are many who had that first connection who have become known around the world – Jack Ma, Founder of Alibaba, was one of our

Leaders of Tomorrow, as was Kira Marie Peter Hansen, the youngest member of the European Parliament."

What does sustainable and systemic change look like for you, in terms of best outcomes, over the next decade?

Beat: "What we need most is a change of attitudes. We see some change, but we need even more change of attitude in politics and business. It's what we want to foster with our Symposium formats, for example, with the latest level of the New Generational Contract, or with Young Leaders on Board, as a platform for young people to be involved in the strategic decision making of companies. We're also discussing with the local government here about bringing in the next generation in their planning."

Nadine: "You touched on an important point in the *context* of change. A lot of times, young people come into organisations with super high ambitions, and you get caught up in the short-term cycles. I used to think failure to think long term is a failure of character, but I realise incentives in the workplace make you think shorter term. If you are the CEO and have to close books and have a yearly cycle, it's too short-term. What it *does* mean is that those people who *can* make the change show extraordinary courage. It is also being true to your principles."

Sophia: "I agree with this tension with the short-term. In so many cases it is about shifting the incentives we currently have."

Richard: "Every 10-year plan needs to have an everyday mindset, where actions count towards it every day."

As practitioners of cross-generational collaboration, what piece of advice would each of you give?

Beat: "Lead with the next generation in mind. Lead with that vision in mind. And reflect on your decisions through that lens every day."

Nadine: "That's perfect from Beat. I would add – don't be afraid to say that you're wrong or need to change course. There is also strength in that as a leader."

Richard: "Learn to listen."

Sophia: "We need braver spaces. We have a problem in many contexts with fault and blame. We need to change the language."

Felix: "I think of the concept of temporal work in academia – especially in strategy, which lives in stories, and the practice of narrating. Temporal means that every organisation has a rich history, a rich archive, and telling that story is important, in how it connects generations past, present and future."

FAST FACTS
ST GALLEN SYMPOSIUM

Platform:	Cross-generational platform, programme and ecosystem
Geography:	Global
Industries:	All
Launched:	1969 (with the first Symposium in 1970)
Purpose:	Lead with the next generation in mind
Composition:	Organisation and network wide

THE EUROPEAN COMMISSION AND PARLIAMENT

Embracing the extremities

Brussels

Seizing the opportunities and addressing the challenges of multigenerational workplaces at scale is something that both the EU Commission and Parliament have been progressive in recognising and realising. These two complex and fascinating organisations have a Venn-like intersection in their purposes and daily interactions. And the context of the organisations, as we outline below, is key to understanding the drivers and dynamics across their multigenerational workplaces. The Treaty of Rome in 1957 established the European Economic Community aimed at achieving European co-operation between six countries. The European Parliament was founded in 1958, and the EU was progressively enlarged so that there are now 27 member states, with approximately 450 million citizens. **The EU Parliament** is the EU's only directly elected institution whose members are elected by voters in all Member States to represent people's interests with regard to EU law-making and to make sure that other EU Institutions are working democratically. The EU Parliament employs about 10,000 staff. **The EU Commission** is much bigger with around 30,000 staff whose role is to instigate and implement EU policies. Its work is led by the Commission's President and steered by the College of Commissioners, drawn from each Member State.

In conversation with **Géraldine Dufort, Principal Adviser Diversity & Inclusion, EU Commission, Chiara Malasomma, Head of the Strategic HR planning unit of DG Personnel, EU Parliament and Chiara Tamburini, Head of the Equality, Inclusion and Diversity Unit of DG Personnel, EU Parliament.**

Géraldine: "The EU Commission is a career organisation, where civil servants starting out in the career system can make it all the way to the top as Director General (DG). Over the past years, we have seen the average age of Commission staff rise, particularly since the 2008 EU financial crisis. Therefore, an important objective of our 2022 HR Strategy is to make sure we attract and recruit younger staff. Another key objective for our staff is to reflect the diversity of the EU population which we serve including younger generations. To do so, we rely on our Blue Book traineeship program which welcomes 2,000 young people per year in the various departments of the Commission, developing a better understanding of career tracks in the EU civil service and encouraging them to apply to our open competitions."

The EU Parliament's multigenerational workforce

Age Range	Proportion of Workforce
20–29	10%
30–39	14%
40–49	38%
50–59	30%
60+	8%

The EU Commission's multigenerational workforce

Age Range	Proportion of Workforce
20–29	4%
30–39	17%
40–49	37%
50–59	34%
60+	8%

The Parliament's Schuman Training Programme is legendary – could you share with us what it is and what makes it so distinctive?

Chiara M: "The traineeships are named after Robert Schuman, one of the main architects of the European integration project, and can be undertaken in Brussels, Luxembourg and Strasbourg or in one of our Liaison Offices in the Member States. Trainees represent about half of the 20–29-year-olds in the Parliament. The aim from our perspective is to provide around 800 high potential young people a year with an insight into the work of the EU Institutions and the European Parliament, and the influx of such a high number of young people twice a year is both refreshing and invigorating. From the young person's perspective, it is also designed to enhance their education and to provide vocational training. Traineeships can be undertaken in a wide variety of fields such as EU internal and external policies, finance, law, multilingualism, administration, logistics, communications or Information Technology, and last for five months."

"The Schuman Recruitment and Development Programme also creates a pathway for a number of high performing trainees to continue working for Parliament, following the successful completion of their traineeship. It's a big commitment from the organisation to do all of this, not just for those involved in the recruitment and selection but also from the host managers and teams throughout the organisation as well as the members of Parliament who interact and spend time with them. And we learn so much from them. They challenge our thinking, help us to better understand how the next generations are thinking. It also gives us a sense of fulfilment from supporting them with the transition from education to the workplace."

"How we think about the extremities is important."

In what you have talked about as a 'career institution', how do you look at the shared value between older and younger generations?

Chiara T: "We have almost as many over 60s as we do under 30s, with Millennial and Gen X representation in the workforce being the largest, with forty somethings at 38% and fifty somethings at 30%. The flexible career paths involving moving roles every seven years helps. Our management training includes explicit elements where younger and older generations are working together. An example of this is the training for new managers, most of whom will be leading some people in their teams who are older than they are. It's important that everyone in a management role is able to relate, to inspire, motivate and manage people no matter what generation they are from, just as with any other form of diversity. How we think about the extremities is important."

Géraldine: "An example of the extremities is where we put more focus on the last 5–10 years before retirement. Our objective is to encourage a positive intergenerational dynamic through the mutual transfer and exchange of knowledge and experience. As another example, The Youth Sounding Board is in line with the work the Commission has done over the years towards a wider consultation. This board is set in that context to get wider feedback from the population of the EU to develop the policies that will have the influence and impact. And there is a big focus on education and culture. What is important to us is bridging the gaps – a mutual bridging through complementary skills and experience. It's a transfer of knowledge both ways."

An insight that resonates throughout our conversation is a culture of curiosity. We would love to get your own perspectives on this.

Géraldine: "We are an institution of polyglots where it is very frequent to have people fluent in 5–6 languages. We have a very strong culture of curiosity in each other and each other's cultures and backgrounds. It is through that will and willingness to understand others in a respectful way that diversity is valued. It's important that this mutual understanding and respect is true for age as well."

Chiara T: "Our culture of curiosity, which we share with the Commission, is an important binding element for us. We are, and have been, since our formation, a highly multicultural workforce, where people are inherently curious and interested in our different cultures, languages and perspectives. We think about all of this in an intersectional way, and age is simply another important aspect of diversity. It's very organic."

"Time present and time past
Are both perhaps present in time future,
And time future contained in time past."

T.S. Eliot

Part of the Four Quartets, *Burnt Norton* was written by one of the most daring innovators of twentieth century poetry. T.S. Eliot was awarded the Nobel Prize in Literature "for his outstanding, pioneer contribution". **As we explore pioneering work in service of future generations, his words are deeply resonant for how we understand the intrinsic connection between generations past, present and future.**

8

Generations Future

So far, we have explored five generations at work in the working world of today. But what about future generations? The challenges and change that we are faced with today, from geopolitical, to climate, to technological, are happening at an unprecedented pace and scale. As volatility and uncertainty become the new normal, adaptability is going to become ever more vital to that agenda, along with the recognition that it is a shared agenda. And that requires greater agility in learning from and with each other, and more collaborative and collective action. It also needs perspective and judgement.

As we explore some of the far-reaching work whose purpose is to encode and protect the lives of future generations, the words of T.S. Eliot seem to be a compelling accompaniment to this chapter, as we reflect on the implications of actions across generations past, present and future. As members of every generation in society today, the generational discourse and our frame of reference tends to focus on time present, informed by time past. If we open the aperture, we afford a different perspective on how we situate ourselves, and on how we choose to act today for the benefit of future generations.

The premise of this chapter is to look at generational trajectories over a longer term. If we are truly to think about why and how businesses and organisations are creating value for the long term, we need to look at how they are evolving in the context of today's five generational workplace, while considering the impact on generations to come. It is something that we heard either explicitly, or implicitly, in every conversation and throughout our research – as evidenced from André Hoffmann's commitment to the 100-year timescale, to Nadine Merz on the tension between short-term business reporting cycles and longer-term imperatives, to the 'good ancestors' philosophy driving the Youth Advisory Board of Imaginable Futures. It is a perspective that is worth us reflecting on, if we are to consider the influence and impact of the systemic change that we are outlining, and advocating for, in this book.

Let us track back to our chapter "Defining Our Generations", in which we charted the projected trends in the size and proportion of the world's populations made up by Gen Alphas, Gen Zs, Millennials, Gen Xers and Boomers from the 2020s to 2050. Millennials and Gen Zs together will make up the majority of the working population over that time, and, as the preceding generations retire, will take on the majority share of decision-making. These are the aggregate global numbers, and as we have seen from the regional summaries, the pace of change differs significantly from region to region and is most dramatic in Africa. However, this is about a lot more than simply how the mix of generations at work will change over the next 25 years. It is also about how ambitious we want – and need – to be in taking action now to maximise our organisations for our collective future.

In a United Nation's policy brief, *To Think and Act for Future Generations*, issued in 2023, the rising commitment to future generations is about hardwiring actions at better service of systemic and sustainable change: "*What most of these models have in common is that they seek to combine knowledge with action, by attempting to understand the future impact of our choices today, and to put that understanding at the service of decision makers.*" The Future Generations (Wales) Act is a world-first that we learned about through Sophie Howe and one that we unpack in our featured conversation. As the rights of future generations are being recognised by a number of country constitutions, including Brazil, Germany, Hungary, Norway and others, the Welsh Government has been the first in the world to appoint a Future Generations Commissioner, a position which Sophie held as the inaugural Commissioner, with the torch being carried forward by Derek Walker. The purpose of the Future Generations Act is designed to integrate future generations as part of the decision-making framework of government today – a compelling story that we go on to unpack in our in-depth conversation. Reflecting on the ideological tensions that we charted earlier in the chapter "Intergenerational Working", the progressive work at constitutional levels takes on a different dimension. As the FT's John Burn-Murdoch reinforces: *"Too often young people's views are overlooked owing to their low rates of political participation, but this shift could leave ripples for generations to come, impacting far more than vote counts."*[1]

A longer now

'How can we become the good ancestors that future generations deserve?' is the question and call to action, posed by Roman Krznaric in his TED Talk *How to be a good ancestor?* He states: *"Over the past decade, a global movement has started to emerge of people committed to decolonizing the future and extending our time horizons towards a longer now. This movement is still fragmented and, as yet, has no name. I think of its pioneers as time rebels."* It is a deeper and wider sense of perspective that is common to the body of work that we have researched and evidenced, and to the progressive thinking behind it. A perspective that is about two-way dialogue, and that is enabled and amplified by generosity and empathy – ultimately, by the ability to walk in someone else's shoes.

As Roman speaks to "a longer now", one of the longer trajectories of work across generations is led by The Long Now Foundation. Their purpose is to foster long-term thinking and encourage imagination at the timescale of civilisation — a timespan that they call 'the long now'. Their work encompasses deep commitments such as: The Organisational Continuity Project, learning from the world's longest-lived organisations to build a discipline of shareable knowledge for our future; and The Rosetta Project, a global collaboration of language specialists and native speakers working to build a publicly accessible digital library of human languages.

> **"... we need to make sure that we are using more knowledge both from young people and from the elders. Vertical thinking is important, but the future I see is in more horizontal connections ..."**
>
> Julia Tscherrig, The SDG Lab at UN Geneva

As a multi-stakeholder innovation space for the SDGs and long-term sustainability, the SDG Lab at UN Geneva is a useful reference point for the thinking that drives decision-making and actions around good ancestry. As Julia Tscherrig, Junior Professional Officer and Strategic Planning Focal Point of the SDG Lab at The UN articulates: *"Political and electoral systems should be designed to prioritise long-term thinking, legacy and behaviour, regardless of the length of the term of office. It is also crucial to preserve, promote, and build on Indigenous Peoples' knowledge systems, cultures and traditional practices, such as the Seventh Generation Principle in Native American culture, which contributes to sustainable and equitable development and the proper management of the environment in a systemic way."*[2]

This Seventh Generation Principle is based on the premise that the decisions that we make should be for the benefit of the seventh generation, thereby challenging and stretching our perspective. This and other versions of the concept, that are expressed differently through different cultures, is something that we have heard contextually through many of the case studies and examples of progressive thinking.

Speaking with Julia Tscherrig in Geneva, we were able to go deeper into the purpose and work of The UN SDG Lab. *"We are focused on key enablers of long-term sustainable development and intergenerational equity. We therefore focus on intergenerational impact and future generations, including how we make decisions that will have mutual benefit for our generations today, as well as accounting for the needs and rights of future generations. Another focus area is regenerative development and sustainable futures, and here we are looking at how we might go beyond GDP. I think of this famous quote of Joseph Stiglitz who said: 'What we measure affects what we do, and if we measure the wrong thing, we will do the wrong thing.' This is also about bringing concepts from the margins to the centre. A third area is on how culture, emotion, beliefs, behaviours, and how values impact long-term sustainability. It's about recognising the importance of values and emotions for acting in a sustainable way. Many people are experts on specific SDGs – we are more focused on the holistic framework of how the SDGs are connected, and how we have a long-lasting impact beyond 2030."*

We talk about the multigenerational workplace and connecting its productivity opportunity with the imperative to regenerate our world, a key part of which, for Julia, is finding a common language across generations. *"I feel that communication between generations often remains a gap. While we at the SDG Lab at UN Geneva are working on intergenerational collaboration, it can be hard at a wider level within the multilateral system to include youth and elders. And this is important, because we need to make sure that we are using more knowledge both from young people and from the elders. Vertical thinking is important, but the future I see is in more horizontal connections and ways of seeing."*

These horizontal connections have an echo in *'an intergenerational chaining effect'*[3] – something that Richard Fisher reminds us of in his book *The Long View*. And this is where we get deeper into the relationship between generations and culture, and the lessons that they can extend across cultures, as he goes on to talk about a Japanese practice called Future Design. *"Led by the economist Tatsuyoshi Saijo of the Research Institute for Humanity and Nature in Kyoto, it involves asking people to wear ceremonial robes that place them in the shoes of future generations when weighing up the pros and cons of policies. This simple ritual has been shown to change how they think."*[4]

And this is part of what matters in intergenerational thinking, in how it deepens our sense of perspective, and the ability to step into the shoes of others. In the case of the Future Design practice in Japan, it is through the act of putting on ceremonial clothes that people are asked to project their thinking. There seems to be something important in this very act, in its tangibility, in this process of making things manifest that we can carry forward and apply to how we think and act more inclusively, as generations today. We talk about the imperative of empathy in so many contexts and respects – this is an act of empathy. Given the pace and dimensions of flux that we are experiencing at the intersection of ageing populations, putting ourselves in the shoes of future generations is a powerful metaphor for how we might look to work more effectively together, today.

The crisis of craftsmanship and lessons from Japan

As we have seen in our conversations with family businesses, Japan is a heartland of some of the oldest family businesses in the world. This is a country facing enormous challenges across its ageing population, challenges that are further projected in the Population Pyramid. This is also a culture that holds extraordinary reverence for its culture of craftsmanship, many examples of which are centuries old. And, like other countries and cultures, it is facing its own crisis of craftsmanship, in the risk of losing this transfer of unique knowledge from generation to generation.

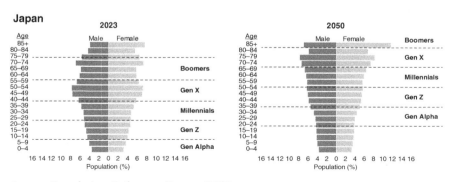

Source: Population Reference Bureau 2023

Living National Treasures, known as "Ningen Kokuho", hold a unique place in Japanese culture, as a lifetime recognition of masters in various fields of art, crafts and performing arts – from ceramics and pottery, lacquerware, woodwork and textiles, to dance, drama, Kabuki and Noh theatre, and music. This unique recognition by the Japanese government began in 1950 and continues today with a maximum of 116 artisans in tenure. Such is the regard for these crafts and skills that some are also recognised by UNESCO as part of the Intangible Cultural Heritage of Humanity.

At the crux of this cultural recognition are the criteria related to being granted the status of a Living National Treasure, which is about a responsibility to generations past, present and future. The honour recognises an artisan's or artist's exceptional achievement and contribution to their respective field. But it also goes far beyond it – the honour is only bestowed on the understanding of an individual's ability and responsibility to transfer their knowledge and expertise to the next generations.

What the Living National Treasures demonstrates is a mutual respect for mastery. There is a value placed on the accumulation of knowledge and expertise that we can learn from in better practices of knowledge transfer within companies and organisations. And we heard this challenge expressed at scale in our conversation with the EU Commission and EU Parliament. We heard parallels with family businesses in the context of maintaining the balance of tradition and innovation. As we discuss the whole notion of how knowledge and skills are carried forward from one generation to the next, a national practice in Japan gives us another valuable lens on how we might look at valuing mastery in business and, crucially, the transfer of that mastery to the next generation.

This transfer of creative knowledge and expertise from one generation to the next is also deeply relevant in the context of the crisis of craftsmanship faced in some areas of the creative industries. A telling headline in The Business of Fashion by Joan Kennedy, sets out one of the biggest skills gaps facing the luxury and fashion industries: *"Bottega Veneta's most consequential launch this Fall may not be a garment sent down the runway, but a new school for craftsmanship."* The creative industries rely on highly specialist skills, some of which originate with founder-family businesses. Many of these creations, whether in the form of accessories, fashion, jewellery or watches, take time in the making. And it is time that presents a pressing challenge for the luxury industry – these skills and this knowledge are at risk of dying out as generations get older, at a time when younger generations are gravitating away from artisanal careers that require a longer-term commitment to mastery of knowledge and skills.

This is why we are seeing a rise in companies investing in state-of-the-art academies. As part of the growing investment by luxury brands in the ongoing preservation and development of skills, Bottega Veneta is amongst the brands investing in the transfer of knowledge and skills, opening The Academia Labor et Ingenium to train new generations of artisans in the brand's "heritage, techniques and craft know-how – savoir-faire". Importantly, the Academy guarantees employment at the culmination of each cohort. As Joan Kennedy states: *"The need is dire. At the end of 2022, 20,000 artisan-led jobs were left unfilled in France."* The estimate for Italy is even higher over the next three years with *"94,000 technical positions left open."*[5]

As we have seen with so much of the work that we have documented, where investments are made through the lens of intergenerational thinking, they tend to have a wider halo effect, through the compound effect of their influence and impact. In London, 'NewGen' was the catalyst for supporting young designers in the fashion industry. Over three decades, 300 designers have taken part in the NewGen scheme, which was celebrated in its anniversary year in the 2023 exhibition at London's Design Museum. Susanna Lau provides a sense of the importance and impact of NewGen, both for the UK fashion industry, and beyond: *"NewGen's high points came in the early-to-mid 2010s when participants like Christopher Kane, Jonathan Anderson and Erdem Moralıoğlu came to full fruition and were being touted as future creative directors of major brands as well as builders of new British houses."* *"Along the way, NewGen itself earned global recognition, inspiring similar schemes, funds, prizes and other initiatives all around the world. Even today, NewGen is the backbone of London Fashion Week."* This is an important point in the context of how these commitments matter. As we discuss throughout the book, we see some refreshing approaches to measurement. And we see it here with how NewGen has been valued, not only for its impact locally, in London, but for the effect that it has had as a catalyst for inspiring other programmes and investment around the world.[6]

This wider halo effect leads us into a deeper dive into a world-first, in pioneering work that is at the service of more effective intergenerational thinking today, for the benefit of future generational outcomes. Importantly, this is hardwiring regeneration across generations, as we go on to unpack in our conversation with the world's first Future Generations Commissioner.

Through this transitional era that we are in, our hope is a new renaissance in the making powered by all generations, collaborating on the major challenges that we face in business, society and as humanity. Edified by the pioneering and progressive work that we are evidencing, with many more stories behind it, a momentum is building. Our will is to channel that momentum into collective action towards more sustainable and systemic solutions.

THE FUTURE GENERATIONS
ACT WALES

Small and awesome
Solving for Systemic Change

Cardiff, Wales

Stories of positive and progressive influence and impact that grow quietly and go on to achieve global recognition hold that extra spark of interest and inspiration. The Future Generations Act (Wales) is a world-first designed with a longer-term vision around generational equity. Based on a set of Ways of Working: Long-term; Integration; Involvement; Collaboration and Prevention, it operates in service of a collective of Well-Being Goals.

We spoke with **Sophie Howe, the first Future Generations Commissioner in the world.**

Sophie, you held a world-first, in being appointed as Future Generations Commissioner for Wales. How did it begin? And what are the biggest insights and lessons from your founding tenure?

Wales has a relatively young Parliament, formed in 1999 after a referendum. In that Government Act, it stated that sustainable development should be a central organising principle. It was a great ambition, but in real terms meant very little. At the time, I was an advisor to two of their first Ministers. And, as with so many missions in the world, this began from a frustration that was growing with one of our

Environment Ministers – Jane Davidson. The frustration was that we were not living up to that big ambition.

What Jane did next was the turning point – she travelled the world and looked at best practice in small nations. And there is a lot of common ground here with this league of small and awesome nations who have the agility to be more progressive. She also built relationships with NGOs and with people who are constructively critical of the Government. It's an important thread of leadership that I also believe in. That's something that really matters to me and to how we get things done – how you find those people who are ready to move things with you.

Jane orchestrated a push that resulted in bringing into being what we're talking about today. We held a national conversation – "the Wales we want" – and engaged citizens around a big question: "What was the Wales legacy that they wanted to leave behind?" That formed the seven well-being goals. The Future Generations Act came into being in April 2016 as a unique piece of legislation, effected as part of the SDGs, and permeates every aspect of what everyone in Wales does. It's a complete cultural change. At the same time, and this is another key insight to share – it's not pre-scriptive. For me, one of the most important factors was to not obsess over the process. Instead, this was about finding ways to lift people up and out. It was about asking questions and engaging in very practical terms around what this means in the context of your citizenship of Wales. For example – what does this mean if you're a doctor, a town planner, a social worker?

"We focused on finding the frustrated champions."

The early part was inspiring people on the aspiration of the Act, and how to do that in a way that contributes to all seven of those goals. And we focused on finding the 'frustrated champions' – in the public sector especially. We were dealing with a system that's silo based, that's short-term and disconnected. The beauty of the Future Generations Act is to give permission to speak up and engage. This is a statutory duty to think long-term, to integrate, to involve, to collaborate and to prevent. Another practical example that worked well for us was showcasing work, which included both the brilliant stuff that these frustrated champions were doing, alongside the madness of what the system *stops* us doing. Again, the most important lesson through all of this was – don't get bogged down with the process.

And as you look back over that vital founding work, and at Wales today, what is changing?

This gets us into one of the most challenging and important parts of this work. And that's because of how we look at measurement. Our systems are set up for 'We'll measure what matters', but if you do that in the absence of a whole system, it's not otherwise informing sustainable change. So, how are you going to educate your civil servants? What's the cultural change in that?

The Future Generations Act was something that I was able to deploy to make interventions.

We're so obsessed with 'fixing' that we never otherwise shift into a prevent mode, which tackles the problem at its root and longer term. One example on which I challenged was a proposal for building a new road to solve traffic congestion. The Act allowed me to challenge the proposal, which revealed that the proposal didn't meet those goals, and this 'solution' would only have led to further short-term fixes, while the root problem wasn't being addressed. As a result – the project was cancelled and rethought. Over time, within the Transport Department, 51 out of 55 proposals were cancelled and crucial funds diverted. That more sustainable thinking was a result of The Generations Act.

And this is not easy work. This is where there are real issues in leadership, in holding your nerve. Long-term investment is a very different thing, and it takes political bravery. This is why the cultural change work is so important, because unless you do that work and reinforce it, all that will happen is that decisions end up retrofitted to the strategy, with proposals that are not solving for sustainable solutions.

And another platform and programme that you launched as part of The Future Generations Act was the Leadership Academy.

Yes!! It all started in trying to amplify the voice of younger generations. In Wales we have an elected Youth Parliament, we lowered the voting age to 16, and every school has a Youth Council. What we don't know is whether they have direct access to leadership.

Enabling that exchange across generations was really important to us. It was also about finding these potential future leaders – people who would carry the torch for others through having been on this Academy.

We partnered across the public, private and third sectors. And there are a few brilliant things about the programme – the diversity is a key one, across gender and identity. But there's also diversity across professions. For example, we had a young DJ sponsored by The Millennium Centre, an engineer from Arup, and a member of the Arts Council working together. These were people who came together who would never otherwise have come into contact with each other. The other thing that worked well was reverse mentoring – where we paired them with existing leaders.

The Leadership Academy began as an experiment, but already it is one that has reaped a lot of benefits as we look at what that first cohort are doing now. One of the reverse mentors was the Permanent Secretary of the Civil Service in Wales, who has now established a Shadow Board – those future leaders are now on the Shadow Board and are part of the team helping the Welsh Government to drive the culture change and implement it through the system. Another one is the reverse mentor for the CEO of Welsh Football, which led to their first sustainability strategy – Wales Wellbeing – and a first in football in the world, which is looking at football's responsibility in improving the health of the nation.

And as you are working with others with a shared agenda, where is the progressive work being done, and what are you seeing?

I'm currently working on system transformation with governments and institutions, looking at what that means across decision making. In New Zealand, the Infrastructure Commission was one of the things that I was working on. And I was working with Cheryl Doig on Think Beyond, which was fascinating – learning from indigenous thinking is completely aligned with The Future Generations Act.

There's a common pattern with other small nations – again, because they have greater agility. There's also work at The UN level, where the Secretary General has been doing work to embed future generations in The UN infrastructure. There is a Declaration for Future Generations, and we're expecting a UN Special envoy for Future Generations, which has the potential to be very significant.

Coda & Call to Action

Wherever this may find you, thank you for reading.

We hope that our words, and the words of five generations around the world, 'fed energy back and forth and amplified it'.

Because this is just the beginning . . . ! In closing out the last words of the book, we open with a call to action.

In the words of the deeply inspiring people and organisations that we have spoken with:

> *Dare to dare.*
>
> *Lead with the mindset of ownership*
>
> *and with the next generations in mind.*
>
> *Put generational diversity at the head and heart of how we operate,*
>
> *in our small and awesome everyday acts.*
>
> *Because . . .*
>
> *together we can be unstoppable.*

Our mission with *Five Generations at Work* was to break the bias, to open-source everyday solutions to inspire action together for change for good. By evidencing positive, pragmatic and progressive work and denoising the divisive discourse, we wanted to provide something more motivating and meaningful – with relevance for companies and organisations across cultures and industries.

Einstein predicted that we would need a "Quantum leap in human relations" to match the same leap in technology. This will not happen by itself, and we need to move from an "Other" to a "Together" mindset, combining talents and perspectives of all generations at work to conquer global challenges and create new possibilities. There is no one solution – there are many, and, as so much of our work demonstrates, progress is taking place in everyday acts.

The complexity of our times and the problems that we are solving for demand better connected and more cohesive organisations – where difference is not only valued, but has the safe spaces to debate, to collaborate and co-create from the strengths of all perspectives. This is why interdisciplinary thinking, and ways of working, is where some of the most powerful work needs to be done.

As a protected dimension of diversity, age is radically over-stereotyped and undervalued. It is all the more ironic in the complexity of problems that we need to solve for in business and society, which require us to realise the very strength that we have in our generational diversity.

These solutions will not be without challenges – they require investment, they require mutuality and a learning mindset. And we have spotlighted some trusted tools and ways of working to counter those challenges. Importantly, these solutions are delivering on influence and impact and sustainable and systemic change – with almost every one sparked by one individual, or a small collective.

As we have seen, every generation defies singular definition and contains multiples. Through acting together, our generational diversity can be the multipliers that we need in business and society. We have shown some of the shifts that are empowering change, from knowledge hoarding to knowledge sharing, from the models and narratives of superhero leadership to those guided by a moral compass and collaborative leadership. We shine a light on the possibilities of a 'small and awesome' world-first, of the 'power of principles' in a global family business, of what happens when one individual 'dares to dare' and inspires others to do the same.

Our call to action is simple: *Spread the word, adopt those ideas which are relevant to your own context and pioneer new ways of combining the talents and perspectives of the generations working in your own organisations.*

This is our call to action, together – we invite you to share your story, your work that is challenging perceptions, closing gaps and delivering change for good.

Take one idea on. Make it better. And multiply it.

This is not a zero-sum game.

Because it is not a game.

It is the one 'wild and precious life'[1] that we have.

And *how* we win together, for good is about compounding the value and interest of generations past, present and future.

We are five generations at work.

This is how we win together, for good.

With Gratitude

Our heartfelt gratitude to everyone who has been part of the journey towards *Five Generations at Work*. Thank you for being generous with your time, your insights and experiences. Thank you to every voice celebrated – from the brilliant gems of a single quote to the deep magic of our conversations – and we celebrate all the voices in your organisation that you represent.

The act of writing is just the beginning. This is a call to action as individuals, as collectives and as organisations – for change for good, together.

Thank you to our insight and data partners **Quilt.AI** and **the Population Reference Bureau** – for the partnership and proximity that fuelled the far-reaching insight and data that was integral to informing our work. A very special thank you to Anurag Banerjee, Co-Founder and CEO Quilt.AI and to your team across Boston, London and Singapore. Quilt.AI was born at the intersection of anthropology and AI, using culturally intelligent machine learning models to study human behaviour, patterns and narratives. A very special thank you to Jeff Jordan and Toshiko Kaneda at the Population Reference Bureau in Washington for your incisive work on demographic data and trends. PRB is a non-partisan research organisation focused on improving the health and wellbeing of people globally through evidence-based policies and practices. Words are about the confluence of truth and beauty, and we wanted to honour them in a cover design that holds its own story. A very special thank you to the world-leading Jason Hyde for designing our book cover, for your extraordinary expertise in type and graphic design and the shared passion in pushing the boundaries.

A cascade of thanks to some special people for your belief and support, which lives on in some of our deeply human conversations: Arlo Brady, CEO Freuds Group, Chairman of the Blue Marine Foundation and Co-Chair of the S30 – a group of the world's leading Chief Sustainability Officers convened by HM King Charles III; Céline Sanzey, Chief Brand Officer LVMH Gaïa; Paul Webber, Brussels-based Senior Advisor for high growth and social ventures; Steve Varley, former UK Chair of EY and former EY Global Head Sustainability.

And with deep thanks to our publisher. Our multigenerational team at Wiley has been more than a publisher; they have been partners. As a 200-year strong legacy brand that remains family-governed, they are a force for sustained innovation, and we were inspired by working with a business that has operated across generations, and champions "the seekers, the changemakers, the innovators. Those who see knowledge as a force for good."

Sources & Notes

Introduction & Call to Action

1. Deloitte (2021). Managing the Multigenerational Workplace.
2. WEF (2020). How a Multigenerational Workforce is Key to Economic Growth.
3. OECD (2020). Promoting an Age-inclusive Workforce.
4. Daniel Jolles, Odessa Hamilton and Grace Lordan (2023). Generational divides: the do's and don'ts of generational labels. *The California Management Review*.
5. London Interdisciplinary School website.
6. Cian O. Morain and Peter Aykens (Gartner researchers) (2023). *Employees Are Losing Patience with Change Initiatives*. HBR.
7. Olisaokafor, P. (2023). Building intergenerational collaboration and leadership in transforming education systems. Cambridge Partnership for Education.
8. Margaret Heffernan (2023). *Success Is More Complicated than One Exceptional Individual*. The Financial Times.
9. Bobby Duffy (2021). *Generations*. Atlantic Books, p. 241 and p. 261.
10. The Seventh Generation principle recurs throughout and is referenced in more detail in the chapter Generations Future.

Defining Our Generations

1. Essays on the sociology of knowledge, Mannheim, K., London: Routledge & Kegan Paul, 1952. Cited in Lyons, S. and Kuron, L., 2014. Generational differences in the workplace: A review of the evidence and directions for future research. *Journal of Organisational Behaviour*, 35(S1), pp. S139–S157.

2. The Federal Reserve Bank of St Louis.

3. Chloe Berger (2023). *Meet the typical Fortune 500 CEO: A total Gen Xer*. Fortune magazine.

4. John Burn-Murdoch (2023). A new global gender divide is emerging. The Financial Times.

5. Deloitte (2023). Gen Z and Millennial Survey.

6. The World Population Prospects: The 2022 Revision, published by The UN Department of Economic and Social Affairs.

7. World Development Indicators database, World Bank, 2023.

8. Demographics of African Faculty, ESSA (Education Sub-Saharan Africa).

9. U.S. Bureau of Labor Statistics projections.

10. Christian Davies, Song Jung-a, and Kang Buseong (2024). $75,000 for a baby? South Korean businesses float incentives as demographic crisis looms. The Financial Times.

11. Alec Russell and Mercedes Ruehl (2023). Is Indonesia finally set to become an economic superpower? The Financial Times.

12. European Commission (2023). Employment and Social Developments in Europe Report.

Intergenerational Working

1. Bobby Duffy (2021). *Generations*, Atlantic Books.
2. The Institute of Fiscal Studies (2023). *Living Standards, Poverty and Inequality.*
3. John Burn-Murdoch. (2024). A new global gender divide is emerging. The Financial Times.

The Intrapreneurial Mindset

1. McKinsey Author Talks with Tomas Chamorro-Premuzic, on *I, Human,* HBR Press, 2023.
2. Meredith Somers (2018). *Intrapreneurship Explained.* MIT Sloan Management Review.
3. Pierre Azoulay, Benjamin F. Jones, J. Daniel Kim, and Javier Miranda. (2020). *Age and High Growth Entrepreneurship*. American Economic Review.
4. *How collaboration and creativity is nurtured cross-functionally at On, Business of Fashion Studio,* 2023.
5. WEF (2023). *Social Intrapreneurship needs an upgrade,* Social Intrapreneur systems.
6. What is Intrapreneurship? Ericsson ONE – website.
7. Forbes (2022). *Women Innovators, Intrapreneur or Entrepreneur, Rani Yadav-Ranjan.*
8. *Unleashing our Superpower. Ericsson's Bold Bet on Intrapreneurship*, Daniel Alexus Head of Ericsson ONE – website.
9. *Unleashing our Superpower. Ericsson's Bold Bet on Intrapreneurship*, Daniel Alexus, Ericsson ONE Launched Ventures – website.
10. Forbes (2022). *Women Innovators, Intrapreneur or Entrepreneur, Rani Yadav-Ranjan.*

11. *Unleashing our Superpower. Ericsson's Bold Bet on Intrapreneurship*, Daniel Alexus, Ericsson ONE Launched Ventures – website.

12. Phocuswire (2017). *Accor Hotels roots ideas in the business through Gen Y.*

13. KPI (Key Performance Indicator).

Family Businesses

1. Tharawat (2019). *Japan's Four Oldest Family Businesses.*

2. Julius Baer Insights (2023). *The Oldest Family Businesses and Why They Lasted.*

3. EY and University of St Gallen Global Family Business Index.

4. Alex Hill, Liz Mellon, and Jules Goddard (2018). *How Winning Organizations Last 100 Years.* HBR.

5. James, H.D. (2022). *Wrestling with legacy in a family business.* HBR.

6. Naini Thaker and Naandika Tripathi (2023). *From Wagh Bakri to Vadilal: How Gujarat's next-gen is reshaping family businesses.* Forbes India.

7. Mars website.

8. Zoe Suen (2023). *Why luxury giants are obsessed with small Japanese suppliers.* Business of Fashion.

9. Forbes (2023). *Mars strategy to double snacking revenues.*

Next Generation Boards

1. Alison Taylor, LinkedIn post.

2. *Marco Bizzarri on how Gucci's Company Culture Fuels Business Success*, The Business of Fashion, 2018.

3. Interbrand's Annual Best Global Brands report.
4. *Gucci's Secret to Success? A Shadow Committee of Millennials*, W Magazine, 2017.
5. *How a century-old luxury brand like Gucci won over Gen Z*, Fast Company, 2019.
6. RenewableUK website.
7. RenewableUK website.
8. EU Commission website.
9. EU Commission website.
10. EU Commission website.
11. Sunnie J. Groeneveld (2023). *Younger people must be given a place in the boardroom.* I by IMD.
12. The 30% Club is a global campaign led by Chairs and CEOs taking action to increase gender diversity at board and executive committee levels.
13. Financial Times data 2023.
14. FT website/ careers blog

Intergenerational Alliances

1. Thomas Friedman (2023). *We are Opening the Lids on Two Giant Pandora's Boxes.* The New York Times.
2. OECD (2020). Promoting an Age-inclusive Workforce.
3. Standard Chartered website.
4. James Root, Andrew Schwedel, Mike Haslett, and Nicole Bitler, Bain (2023). *Better with Age Report.*
5. Emily McCrary-Ruiz-Esparza (2023). *Families taking a new family leave – for grandparents.* Quartz.
6. *The Performance Prism: The Scorecard for Measuring and Managing Business Success*, Pearson Education 2002.

7. R. Edward Freeman (2010). *Strategic Management: A Stakeholder Approach*. Cambridge University Press.
8. OECD (2020). Promoting an Age-inclusive Workforce.
9. Imaginable Futures website.
10. Imaginable Futures Website.
11. Imaginable Futures Website.
12. *Denken und Handeln, Sieglinde Geisel* (translated) 125 Jahre Universität St Gallen.

Generations Future

1. John Burn-Murdoch. (2024). *A new global gender divide is emerging*. The Financial Times.
2. UN SDG Lab (2023). Safeguarding Rights of Future Generations for Long-term Sustainability.
3. Richard Fisher (2023). *The Long View*. Hachette, p. 101. The 'intergenerational chaining effect' was *proposed by the philosophers Tyler M. John and William MacAskill*.
4. Richard Fisher (2023). *The Long View*. Hachette, p. 101.
5. Joan Kennedy (2023). *Fashion's Craftsmanship Challenge*. Business of Fashion.
6. Susanna Lau (2023). *The legacy of London's original young designer support scheme*. Business of Fashion.

Coda & Call to Action

1. Mary Oliver

Bibliography

You will find direct references made in the book within the Sources & Notes section. In complement to that we have outlined a selection of some of the many articles, books, podcasts, reports and studies that we have drawn on. If you are looking for more information or inspiration on a given topic, please feel free to get in touch with us.

Age Diversity / Intergenerational

Better with Age, The Rising Importance of Older Workers, Report by Bain, 2023

Beyond Z, Report by Channel 4, 2023

Bring Younger Employees into the Leadership Ranks, HBR, 2023

Diverse teams feel less comfortable and that's why they perform better, Rock, Grant and Grey, HBR

Four Quarters podcast, Avivah Wittenberg-Cox

Generational Divides, Daniel Jolles, Odessa Hamilton, and Grace Lordan, California Management Review, 2023

Generation Z, How to Recruit and Retain Them, Jonathan Black, FT, 2022

Gen Z & Millennial Survey, Deloitte (2022; 2023)

Generations, Bobby Duffy, Atlantic Books, 2021

Global Human Capital Trends Survey, Deloitte

Harnessing the Power of Age Diversity, HBR, 2022

How to Manage a Multigenerational Team, Emma Waldman, HBR, 2021

How to Manage a Multigenerational Workforce, Northbay Business Journal

In Search of Chief Executives Who Never Grow Old, Andrew Hill, FT, 2023

Promoting an Age Inclusive Workforce, OECD

The Envy at Work That Dare Not Speak Its Name, Pilita Clark, FT, 2023

Tolstoy's Bicycle. Who Did What, When? Jeremy Baker, Helicon, 1995

4 Ways to Help Different Generations Share Wisdom at Work, Chip Conley, HBR, 2018

5 Ways in Which the Workplace Could Serve Young People Better, World Economic Forum, 2023

Intrapreneurship

Age and High Growth Entrepreneurship, MIT and NBER, Pierre Azoulay, Benjamin F. Jones, Northwestern University and NBER J. Daniel Kim, MIT Javier Miranda, U.S. Census Bureau, 2019

The Best Examples of Intrapreneurship in Action, Chartered Management Institute, 2015

Big Companies Must Embrace Intrapreneurship to Survive, George Deeb, Forbes, 2016

Intrapreneuring, Gifford Pinchot III and Elizabeth Pinchot, 1985

Collaboration

Collaborative Circles, Michael P. Farrell, University of Chicago Press, 2021

Collaboration is a key skill, so why aren't we teaching it? MIT

Leveraging the Power of Cross-Generational Teams, Report by The St Gallen Symposium, 2021

The Future of Business, Culture and Work

Anthro-Vision, Gillian Tett, Penguin, 2022
Changing Company Culture Requires a Movement Not a Mandate, HBR, 2017
The Culture Map, Erin Meyer, PublicAffairs, 2014
The Performance Prism: The Scorecard for Measuring and Managing Business Success, Pearson Education 2002
Range, How Generalists Thrive in a Specialised World, David Epstein, Macmillan, 2019
UK Business Values Survey, The Oxford Character Project, The University of Oxford 2023

Family Businesses

Annual Global Family Business Index, EY and The University of St Gallen
Family Business on the Couch, Manfred Kets de Vries and Randel Carlock, with Elizabeth Florent-Treacy, Wiley, 2007

Next Gen Boards

Emerging Talent, Careers Whitepaper, The Business of Fashion, 2021
FTSE Women Leaders Review Report
How to Effectively Engage Your Junior Talent, The Business of Fashion, 2021
How a Century Old Luxury Brand like Gucci Won Over Gen Z, Fast Company, 2019
How Shadow Boards Bridge Generational Divides, HBR, 2022
Millennials in the boardroom, Govenda
Rebel Ideas, The Power of Diverse Thinking, Matthew Syed, John Murray Press 2019

Shadow Boards, Sathnam Sanghera, The Times, 2021
Women on Boards Report, 2022
Why You Should Create a 'Shadow Board' of Younger Employees,
HBR, 2019
*Your Company Needs a Shadow Board of Young Non-Executive
Talent*, Rebecca Robins, Quartz, 2020

Future Generations

The Long View, Richard Fisher, Headline Publishing, 2023
United Nations SDG Lab

Index by Industry & by A-Z

We believe that a book should be as helpful as possible to you in navigating the content that matters most. We have listed the brands, businesses and organisations featured in the book to enable you to find the most relevant content, both by A-Z and with a snapshot by Industry.

Index by Industry

Index by A-Z